CURDELLA FORBES

SONGS OF
SILENCE

Part of Pearson

Heinemann is an imprint of Pearson Education Limited, a company incorporated in England and Wales, having its registered office at Edinburgh Gate, Harlow, Essex, CM20 2JE. Registered company number: 872828

www.heinemann.co.uk

Heinemann is a registered trademark of Pearson Education Limited

Text © Curdella Forbes 2002

First published in Heinemann's Caribbean Writers Series in 2002

Second edition with study notes 2010

14 13 12 11
10 9 8 7 6 5 4 3

British Library Cataloguing in Publication Data.
A catalogue record for this book is available from the British Library.

ISBN 978 0435089 09 2

Designed and typeset by Sara Rafferty
Cover design by Sara Rafferty
Cover illustration © Carlisle Harris
Printed by Multivista Global Ltd

Acknowledgements
Every effort has been made to contact copyright holders of material reproduced in this book. Any omissions will be rectified in subsequent printings if notice is given to the publishers.

CONTENTS

For
Tony and Valrie, who went on before
and Uncle Corny, spinner of tales
because
one day
I know
the silence, open wound
ships' ghosts
will heave to starward,
close

EFFITA

Miss Effie must have been the second oldest person in our district when I was nine. Auntie Sare (short for Sarah) the midwife, was the oldest, she was older than forever, and couldn't help herself any more. She use to walk up and down in her one room house, her hands black and twist up like tree branch tight on the knob of her cotton tree walking stick, her face cross up cross up with wrinkle like Jimbo Gully after November rain. She couldn't see very well, in fact and in truth I not sure she could see at all, but she could feel and smell and hear like anything, she know everybody by how they footstep sound, and if they come near her, like Isaac she know they feel and she know they smell. My mother say is she bring most of the old people in the district into the world, but now she couldn't help herself. So every Sunday either my mother or one of the other women would put dinner in a wares dish (you can't feed a guest in a enamel plate, that is a sign of disrespect or extreme poverty) and wrap the dish in a white embroidered doily, and one of us children would take it carefully down to Auntie Sare, walking careful and slow slow because you didn't want the curry from the chicken to run on the doily. I don't know how she eat during the week, because my mother didn't send anything on those days, so I figure the other women took turn to feed her, same way as on Sundays.

Visiting Auntie Sare was both a treat and a fearful experience. She always had some kind of sweetie in her apron pocket, which she would lavish on you for bringing her dinner, but she also never miss making you sit down and praying for you, long, loudly and in great and explicit detail, as if the Almighty was both deaf and ignorant of what was happening in the district and had to be kept inform by Auntie Sare. I was completely fascinated by the explicitness of Auntie Sare's prayers, because I couldn't understand how she find so much to say and how come so much of what she pray was accurate.

'Our Father-Which-Art-in-Heaven,' she would begin, 'hallowed be Thy most holy and reverent precious name. Lord Massa Jesus, we is not worthy to be call Thy servants, but Thou in Thy mercy has see fit to call us into Thyself that we might have everlasting life. Lord Jesus, look now upon this Your humble servant and this child that I brings before Thee for Thy blessing. Lord You know the poor parents, they do not have it, they do not have it Lord but they trying, they trying hard. Many times Lord, precious Jesus, You look down upon dem and You sees dem, You see how the little food can't barely stretch yet they stretch out the hand to bless the poor such as Thy humble servant, bless them O Lord, and bless the little child strivin in school to do of har best. Sometime no book to read out of Lord, but Thou knowest, and Thou wilt pervide, for You say to us You have the cattle on a thousand hill, the earth is Thine and the fullness thereof, take no heed for tomarra, for tomarra wi tek care of itself, Lord my God ...' and so she would go on, quoting Scripture after Scripture to the Almighty, holding on firmly to the middle top plait of your hair so you couldn't wriggle away (which, unlike the boys, I was always too terrified to do anyway). Auntie Sare had this rusty sort of voice like it coming out of a grave, that scared the daylights out of you, and she would pray louder and louder the longer she pray, so that after a while other children would gather around the doorway to watch and murmur in relay, from the front of the group to the back, 'Is Auntie Sare deh pray fi Marlene again', and somebody would push forward murmuring, 'Mek me look', pushing and shoving and bickering until the prayer was over. Everybody would scatter as soon as Auntie Sare open her eye because they knew she would pray for them too.

'Auntie Sare is a four-eye lady?' I use to ask my mother, confused about her intimate knowledge of our household affairs.

'No,' my mother would say, 'Auntie Sare is a Christian woman, why you always askin me that?'

'She a converter?'

'No, Christian an' converter is not the same thing. Converter more like Revival.'

'She a four-eye though,' I would respond adamantly, unable to explain the basis of my certainty but sure I was right. My mother just gave up, until the next argument.

Effie (all the bigpeople called Miss Effie Effie, so we call her the same behind her back) was very interesting to me because she always cry whenever anybody died. You always knew there was a death because Effie's crying was a kind of public announcement. She would put her apron up over her head, tie her waist with some sort of cloth, and process up from Green Town where she live, weeping and wailing, 'Mumma, ban you belly, mumma, ban you belly, Johnny dead Johnny dead Johnny dead, woie!' We use to live under a banking below the main road where everybody pass to go to Maaga Bay or out of the district. Green Town, which was full of people surname Green (mostly related to us) was about three miles from us in the opposite direction and about two miles from Black Shop, the first of our two piazzas. But we could hear Effie, a distant attenuated wail, from she round the ridge into Black Shop, and my mother would look up from whatever she was doing and say, 'Tap, no Effie dat? Smaddy dead, wonder is who?'

That was our cue, the unwritten permission to go and find out. We would race out of our yard and up the incline to the road, and all around us in other yards other children would be doing the same, and the adults would begin calling out to each other across fences, 'Miss Zetta, Miss Ionie oh, you hear who dead? No? So is how Effie bawling so? Wonder is who, lawd is what dis now.'

Effie's rhythmic chant would increase in volume with the progress of her advance and the paroxysm of her trance. She really did seem to get into a kind of frenzy, a strange wild possession that had her bucking, gyrating and dancing like a dervish as she came, her voice reaching ever new heights of ululation. It was amazing to watch. She hold her waist with her left hand and her hair with her right, and was as if between her waist and her trunk there was no muscle of co-ordination, she was really two bodies that her hand hold together, because she would buck hard from the waist in a rapid series of frantic bows, flinging her head like a rag doll that broke. The louder she chant the faster she buck, until you dizzy just watching her. At intervals she spin and spin and spin, three fast spins in a row, and then the bucking again, tears raining down her face the whole time. Sometimes it seem to me that I hear a thousand crashing drums, a thunderous orchestra of the spirit, beating out their wild accompaniment to the wailing violin improvisations of Miss Effie's cry. It didn't seem as if Miss Effie was alone. I had this feeling of being surrounded, vague vibrating presences coming out of everywhere to stand in circles around us. And the wailing desolate chant, the irresistible incantation, 'Johnny dead Johnny dead Johnny dead, woie!' That's how you knew who had dead. You

4

couldn't ask her at these times how Johnny dead or any of the details, you had to wait until she finish making the round of the district and was on her way back, exhausted, rational and spent, and then the women would stop her to enquire, if the full news hadn't arrive by hot-foot messenger by then.

As soon as the bigpeople could make out whose name Effie was calling, my mother would realize we not in the yard and would begin shouting at us to come there this minute, who sent us on the street, anybody showing you anything? Pickni fast and inquisitive dead bad at sun hot. So for us the show would be quickly over. Most other mothers allowed their children to watch Effie until she disappear. We had to be content with the liminal gift of her voice's vestiges floating behind her towards us out of the distance as she head into Maaga Bay.

Effie didn't confine her activities to our district. She made announcement and attend funeral as far away as Mount Peace, two districts away. That was another thing about Effie. She always attend the funerals she announce, and she cry and shout and mourn with the relatives as if the person who die was her own. I was amazed at the fund and fecundity of her tears.

There was one time Effie made a wrong announcement, and one time she didn't announce at all. The first was the time Chisel Bwoy shoot my cousin Melwyn. Melwyn was strange and important in our district because he had gone to prison and been let out and come back home. Before Melwyn, I had never known anyone who went to prison, and in my mind he was a great mystery and something of a celebrity. I asked my mother what he go to prison for but I can't remember what she say, which means she must have been enormously vague on the matter. My mother was always vague on things she felt

5

you shouldn't know but didn't want to say it out loud in case you get too interested and decide to find out for yourself. Years later I decided it must have been for stealing, since stealing was a major disgrace you didn't want to mention in connection with your family. I ruled out murder because murder is usually worth the telling, surrounded with the kind of drama and rarity that make it sweet to tell. Moreover, you could commit murder for all sorts of exciting reasons, like protest at being unfairly treated or because someone was fooling around with your woman.

The first time I see Melwyn up close was one twelve o'clock when I was going home with my big sister Magsie to eat lunch. Most of us children went home for lunch since school was quite near. Melwyn was leaning up against Miss Zetta shop, talking to some men. I knew it was him because my mother greet him one time when he pass by our gate just as we coming up the incline into the road. Plus he was easy to remember because he looked like his mother, Miss VeenAnn, who was my first cousin, which made Melwyn and us either first cousins once removed or second cousins, I not sure which.

Melwyn was tall and big-shouldered, with a whole heap of coolie royal hair that made me wonder if he was a Rasta, but my mother said no, is just because he was in prison a long time. He was the handsomest man I had ever seen. He had a small purse-up mouth and the rest of his face was straight and clean-boned. I was the kind of child that didn't talk at all, but I was so fascinated with Melwyn that when my sister Magsie say she going to greet him, I didn't protest, though as usual my heart stop with fright how she daring. She grab onto my hand and walk bold and bareface up to the group of men, an action that in itself was a wonder and a terror to me. I try to wriggle away but she hold my hand tight tight so in the end all I could do was to hide my face against her skirt.

'Good evening, Maas Baada, evening Maas Attie.' I hold my breath. 'Good evening, Melwyn.'

'Evenin, sweetness,' drawled Maas Baada, stuffing more tobacco into his pipe, which did smell real bad, 'what a nice mannersly child. Is Barber daughter nuh?'

'Yes, sir,' my sister answered unfazed. 'Mr Melwyn, me and you is cousin you know. By my mother side.'

Melwyn straighten up from where he leaning against the shop. He look down at her from his great height and smile the long slow smile that I always think of him by, all of afterwards. 'Yeah, me know. Is Miss Ionie daughter, don't?'

My sister nod her head to say yes. Melwyn come round her to where I squinting up at him from behind her skirt, do Jesus, what I go do now?

He squat down on the ground and take hold of my hand. 'So what is your name, little cousin?'

I tell him, barely in a whisper.

'Nice,' he say, his eye twinkling down at me.

'Nice. And you are a nice little girl. I hope you studying your book good in school.' And he put a whole shilling, a bright new shilling, in my hand.

'She bright bright,' my sister announce proud proud, as she announce to everyone who care to listen. 'She don't even have to study her book.'

I longed for the earth to open and rescue me but when Melwyn smile at me for the second time and murmur, 'Good, good, nice', I fell in love for the second time in my life. The first was Teddy, who live on the hill above us when I was four and we lived in Somerton St James. Teddy was tall, taller than Melwyn, taller even than Long Man, and he use to ride a

7

horse and he walk very fast when he not riding. When he pass our gate I run out to meet him, shouting his name as loud as I could, and he always stop, no matter how fast he was walking or riding, and he would sit or swing down to talk. I have no idea what we use to talk about except I have a feeling I told him everything, and my mother must did trust him because she never call me back when I run to meet him. Sometimes she let me ride with him on his horse, a big dark brown stallion named Whithorn. We lived on Walcott Hill which belonged to Teddy's family, the Walcotts, who were high brown and very rich. You could tell by the difference between their house and ours. They lived above us on the hill, in a huge mansion surrounded by dogs.

But I'm supposed to be telling you how Chisel Bwoy shoot Melwyn, and Effie bring the wrong news. This particular day Melwyn was hanging out by the shop piazza as usual, talking with the old men who didn't go to the fields because according to my mother, dem well lazy and don't want to work. I wondered if Melwyn, who was young, was lazy too but I never ask, maybe because I didn't think I would too like the answer. Anyway, there they were, laughing and talking as usual and passing round the rum glasses which Miss Zetta keep filling up as fast as they emptying. Miss Zetta had a sign above the shop front saying, '*It is my intention to apply for a licence to sell rum, gin, brandy and other distilled spirits at the next assize of the Court, dated this year of our Lord nineteen hundred and sixty-five.*' According to how Miss Zetta later told the story, Chisel Bwoy, who had just been made District Constable and been issued with a gun, something unheard of in our district – Maas John and Pappa Lazzy were both DCs and we had never seen them with a gun, and only occasionally in their constable's blue-seam uniforms – Chisel Bwoy was trying out his new constable suit and his new gun. He was just coming in from Lucea, and he get off the van in Maaga Bay and walk into Black Shop, saying he looking for Melwyn. No one knew what he and Melwyn had, what sort of secret quarrel, but be that as it may, Chisel Bwoy reportedly march into Black Shop, gun at the ready like him is Errol Flynn or Stewart Granger, and, stopping for nothing and nobody, walk up to Miss Zetta shop, where he advance on Melwyn, demanding, 'Stick 'em up!'

According to Miss Zetta who was inside the shop round the back wrapping salt and saw everything, Melwyn throw up his hands with a frightened look on his face and cry out, 'Don't shoot me! Ah beg you don't shoot me!' Chisel Bwoy shoot him anyway, at point-blank range in the lower left abdomen. Melwyn drop on the ground same time rolling and bleeding, the blood pouring out like river and mudding up the dust in the road. Miss Zetta and the men somehow manage to get Maas Levi, the only person in the district with a car, to bring his Chevrolet to take Melwyn to Lucea Hospital. The Chevrolet was so old and rusty and battered it was always touch and go if it would start, and if it start, you keeping your fingers crossed if it would finish the journey. Some people nicknamed it 'May Reach' but thank God this time it did reach and Melwyn didn't die. I heard they had was to fly him up to UC the wound was so bad, but I don't know how much truth there was in that since is Miss Ida bring the news and it was no secret she tell lie like horse galloping on the road.

Anyway, the point is that Melwyn didn't die. But Effie wasn't to know that. Two twos after Maas Levi car pull out of Black Shop, shooting black smoke and backfire pi pi pi like Caesar's Gallic Wars, and the news hit Maaga Bay, Miss Effie

9

surge up out of Green Town, apron on head, cloth on waist, moaning, weeping and chanting, 'Woie! Woie! VeenAnn, ban you belly, VeenAnn, ban you belly, Melwyn dead Melwyn dead. Melwyn dead, woie-oie!'

'Effie!' Miss Florrie shout from her front verandah next door to our yard, 'Stap de noise, yu too lie! Melwyn no dead, him only get shot but him no dead. How you love mek so much mischief and car' so much news?'

'Yes, car' too much news. Chups!' Her daughter-in-law Miss Julett sucked her teeth loudly and walked off inside the house.

I don't think Effie heard them because she just kept right on going and wailing and bowing and weeping. But only the children gather this time, ever awed and drinking in the high drama of her carryings on. My mother made no permissive comment so we couldn't join in the show, we could only listen from below. It wasn't until she got to Maaga Bay that someone got through to her that she had it all wrong, and by then it was too late. We heard it from good source that when Miss VeenAnn come out on the road and grab Miss Effie in her collarbone and call her quiet and firm by her right name, 'Effita, tap de bawling, no call down no dead pon me pickni, him no dead, doctor seh him wi recover', Effie was utterly devastate, she just sit down braps on the ground at Miss VeenAnn foot, put her arm in her lap and her head on her arm, and cry and cry and cry, weakly in a thin, high voice like a mosquito's keening. For days after, people were laughing.

Melwyn recover and came out of hospital. Nothing happen to Chisel Bwoy, who plead before the court that Melwyn had attack him and refuse to put up his hands when accosted. Years later when he lost a leg and went begging on Barnett Street in Montego Bay, where I often used to see him, smiling and obsequious and impeccable dress, hopping on his wooden leg and his hand stretch out, my mother said it was retribution for the wickedness he had done to Melwyn all that time ago, you think God sleeping, Him don't wear pyjama and if Him even go out, Him know when time to come in.

The time Miss Effie didn't announce was when her nephew Son Son died. Son Son was in my sister's class in school and he use to get fits. When he got an attack you had to put a silver spoon in his mouth crossways so he wouldn't swallow his tongue, but this time apparently nobody was there to put the spoon in his mouth or he start to swallow the tongue before they got the spoon in, or maybe they couldn't find a silver one. Be that as it may, Son Son dead before help could reach him and that was that. The death shake up everybody and especially us children because Son Son was only fourteen and children didn't die in our district. In fact only old people died and they usually do it in threes, one after the other, so the carpenter Maas Rat knew if he make one coffin today, he could prepare to make another tomorrow and another one the day after. What made it worse was Son Son was our cousin – as I said before, everybody in our district was related or almost related. Then to make matters still worse, Miss Herfa and Man Teacher decide to make big announcement and call for minute of silence in school the day after it happen, because Son Son was a pupil of the school. I lost all the excitement that come with death and began to feel like a mourner. It reminded me of the time the Prime Minister dead and the whole district go into mourning, even the PNP supporters, and everybody was saying is some grudgeful member of the party poison him, put cornmeal in rum under they fingernail. He didn't die fast the way people usually bloat up and die when you poison them with cornmeal in rum, instead he linger on in a hospital in Canada for weeks in a coma, haemorrhaging and dying until when it looked like it was really no turning back, the Queen knight him so he die a Sir. People in my district were really proud of him. For days all you could hear going round the district from fence to fence and on the shop piazzas was, 'Middleton get knighthood, you hear? The Queen recognize him is a great man, you don't see?' and it seem to compensate somehow for all the mourning, people's grief was appeased. But I had been drawn into this national grief that was bigger than any mourning I had seen before and suddenly it was like there was a world outside that was coming into our district and my mind. I couldn't explain it but suddenly the world was bigger than I knew it and Government was no longer this big distant person who affected our lives on the edge of dreams and story about Busta, Government was the picture of the dying Prime Minister on Man Teacher office wall that I could stretch out my hand and touch. The picture on Man Teacher office wall wasn't a deathbed picture, it was a nice picture of the Prime Minister, who was a pretty man, in his eyeglasses looking out and smiling. But I used to see the deathbed pictures in the *Gleaner*, which during this time my mother bought every day. I got into the habit of creeping into Man Teacher office every recess to sit and look sorrowfully at the Prime Minister in his well face, and often I would feel the tears stealing down my own face in sadness for what the *Gleaner* said was his untimely death. But mostly I cried because he was a pretty man who had brought into my world a breath from the big and awesome world outside.

Son Son's death was a bit like that – bigger than we

could imagine so we all cried. Effie was nowhere in sight making any announcement, but she must have been among the first to know since they live in the same house. My mother didn't usually let us go to wake and funeral just so because she didn't want us like hootiah on the road like ole naygar pickni, but this time we got to go because the whole school was going.

At the graveside it was really weird because Effie keep very quiet and people start to get uneasy. I was there wondering why she not crying and getting in the spirit and I could see other people looking at her out of their eye corner so I know they thinking what I thinking. And I start to get disappointed. But stop, I talk too soon.

As the pallbearers lower the coffin into the ground and the parson say, 'Dust to dust ashes to ashes' in that voice that make cold bump rise up on your spine with the mystery and the awesomeness of it, Miss Effie go into action. Is like a bullet from a gun go off in her head at the sound of the parson voice. Miss Effie scream out one loud scream fit to wake the dead, and tear off her hat and her shoes and jump down into the grave. Several of the men reach out to catch her but they too late, Miss Effie already face up on the coffin in the hole beating her heels on the top and bawling, 'Jesus Jesus Jesus Hallelujah! Hallelujah Woie! Woie! Woie! Son Son dead Son Son dead Son Son dead Son Son dead, Effie, ban you belly! Ban you belly!'

It take three men to get Miss Effie out of Son Son grave and by that time she and them cover all over with dirt she pull down from the graveside. Some people was really fed up and say is full time Effie stop this foolishness, look how she even go to her own nephew funeral go disrupt and cause disgrace. Some say is jus so Effie stay, you not going get any different, but still is really something eh, for I never see her jump down in the grave before. Usually she make plenty noise and dance up and down like she working obeah round the grave, but you could see she did really love the little boy. It really affect her.

After that, Miss Effie was quiet for a long time. It might have been because nobody die, but I don't really think so because she keep her head down instead of making a lot of noise and singing, the way she use to do when she wasn't announcing.

Miss Effie die in 1995. She must have been at least a hundred. I ask my father but he say he didn't really go to the funeral, and I don't know who else did, so I couldn't ask how it went.

She lived alone in a two-room house on Tam Briscoe Hill. The hill sloped up from the main road by Miss Vie Allen's house and spread out at the top into rolling acres of open grassland pitted with sudden, half-hidden bumps of dark stone: slate, shale – which we called 'bruggudup', because of the sudden abrupt way it had of sheering off and falling in gruff heaps to lower ground – and the hard grey rock that grew in river-beds. It was easy to think the hill had once been part of a river-bed, maybe a waterfall, especially as at the bottom, by Miss Vie's house, the ground pooled into a kind of hollow that during the rainy season exposed its resistance to the asphalt overlay that sought to make it smooth.

The cottage was made of marl stone, with a cone-shaped zinc roof burnt rust and dark ochre by the sun. It had jalousied board windows and a jalousie door which faced outward to the face of the hill, as if it would have engaged in conversation. Except that the shutters were always closed and the front door never open. The door led out to a long narrow verandah that ran all the way around the house like a fence. The floorboards were worn and unpolished, as if whoever cleaned the place felt it was a waste of time to spend dye and good beeswax where the wind and rain would sweep it off in no time at all. The verandah, unlike the rest of the house, was all wood, with fine low railings that you could vault over, but it never invited you to. There was a broken stone Spanish jar in one corner near the front step, but no rocking chairs sat expectantly waiting for inmate or guest. The whole bare expanse of the verandah had a deserted feeling, exaggerated by the loss of the front step, which was half broken down and hidden in tall blond grass like uncombed white people's hair.

But I, who had grown up among ghosts and ruined districts and a woman who sang of death like a tribal griot, was used to presences, and presences were thick beneath the shuttered not-at-home windows and the thick skipping-rope vines that crept like massed fingers up the pale pitted walls of the house. We passed by there in July and August, when school was out, on our way to the bush where my father reaped mango and pimento in the fragrant summers, bagging up most of the pimentos' fine grains for when Mr Briscoe came, keeping back some to sell in Lucea market along with the mangoes so he could make a living.

All the land, including the space where she lived, belonged to Mr Briscoe. My father was the caretaker.

We never spoke to her. She never spoke to us.

Sometimes if it was early morning or late evening when the sun was setting, we would see her wandering on the grassland behind the house, her head bent under its weight of coiled black hair that wrapped her temples like a crown and fell in a thick plait to just above her shoulders. She was thin and high brown like Mr Briscoe, and she always wore a long thin dress in some pale fabric like white dacron. We never saw her face.

Nobody visited. Smoke never rose from the outside kitchen and the door of the outside toilet swung open on its hinges, as if someone wanted the wind to pass through.

There were stories. She was a Briscoe, people said. Go off her head like Netta Purcell and she come back from asylum, lock up by herself in the old Briscoe caretaker house, not talking to anybody.

But where her people?

Oversea. Every one of them gone oversea. Evert Briscoe, the one who own the piece of hill and the land my father

16

look after, was the only one who come home sometime, but he only come to look at his land and make sure Barber not robbing him, he don't care too much about her.

They all throw her off. Every single one of them. For they shame how she mad, Briscoe is high blood and can't brook disgrace. They tell lie about where she go the time she disappear, say is abroad and she never like the cold so she come back, but everybody know is lie, is asylum the girl come from.

There were stories. She make a fool of herself over some man who promise right by her but it turn out he already have a wife in England, and when attaclaps come and he suppose to take her to the altar, he disappear. She never look at a man or talk to anybody since.

She use to go to the Wesleyan church in Baltree district. Nice Christian girl every Sunday in her white choir frock sitting in the parson mouth drinking in everything he say. But even then she was strange. Use to shout and carry on loud loud during the sermon, 'Hallelujah! Hallelujah! Thank you Jesus! Thank you Jesus!' disturbing the peace so is a wonder anybody else in church hear the sermon, and you know Wesleyan people is quiet people, just like Seven Day, don't make noise in church. After church going home she making up noise same way, all the long way on the road, shouting and shivering and weeping, 'Hallelujah! Hallelujah! Glory, Hallelujah, Jesus!' as if she have some great trouble that deeper than the depths of the sea, and no words on the face of the earth could reach but it pumping up with the fountain of her tears. What kind of trouble could a young girl like that have in her tender years? And her people have money.

But one day she just stop going and people found in her place a fountain of silence.

Some say is not so the story go, she cook cucumakka stick and throw away belly, and it go up in her head and make her strange.

There was inbreeding in the family. Them red people think they too good for black people, marry they cousin, they aunt, they uncle, no must produce bad breed? That is the disease eating out the poor girl brain, not no man story.

No, is not so it really go. Not a thing more than the girl want man, but she can't see anybody of her class to marry to, black man not good enough for those kinda people, no? So they prefer stay by theyself even if loneliness make them fart.

How old was she? I did not know, nobody knew. Or how long she had been there.

I had images.

The wild expanse of the grass in the unused pastureland under the setting sun. A thin ghostly face under the shadows of a lifted shutter, peering out at the gloaming, just as the peenie-wallies begin to come out. Peenie-wallie light flicks and blinks all over the grey blond grass. An intimation, a shadow of voices breasting the hill, and the shutter comes abruptly down, the face at the window disappears.

The pale hem of a skirt flashes among naseberry trees at the edge of the pastureland, trembles on the brink of a sudden wind, melts into the undergrowth.

I wonder about graves, and whether she feeds the dead. There are graves all around us, under houses, under crops. From slavery days, my mother said. Sometimes in the river she sees people passing, women with washpans on their heads, processions of men on their way to a digging, forks and cutlasses swinging. Sometimes she hears singing, more than the river's voices. My mother could have been a four-eye woman.

There are graves between the naseberry trees.

Why did nobody go there? People fed Auntie Sare. But you have to understand. This one high brown and stand-offish, wouldn't take anything from anybody. You can't just push up yourself on red people so, they have to invite you first. Moreover, every fourth Thursday she covered her head, came off the hill and went to the post office where Miss Clemmy handed her a register slip which she signed and handed back in return for a letter with six England stamps and a register mark on the left corner of the envelope. Her people in England supported her. Every fourth Thursday at the post office.

Did she speak? On these occasions, did she speak? What did her voice sound like? Or was speech unnecessary, Miss Clemmy already expert in the semiotic of her silence, her downcast head and the imperium of her brownness, which prefigured speech? Could she speak? Or were there sounds, the strangled remains of a ruined utterance, as ruined as the face I imagined but could not see? These were not questions I, as a child and one moreover who did not speak and was not barefaced, could ask Miss Clemmy, and when I asked my mother she simply said, 'Yes, man, she can talk. She jus strange.'

Just strange. So simple a phrase, so open, so transparent in its vowels, but rounding and hiding worlds of meaning I could not decipher. What was strange?

I was strange. When I went to school the children laughed because when they lifted my dress to see whether I was wearing store-bought jersey panties or hand-sewn, homemade cloth ones, I cried. And when anybody looked at me too hard I cried. I cried because the teacher forced me to say good morning so that I was seen. This was the morning I came late and lost my camouflage, the other children I could slip in behind and hide in the general chorus, 'Morning Miss Nelson!' making sure my voice was not heard.

I understood silence. I understood the stone prison and the snail's secret house of being unable to speak. For me, from the day I went to school until I changed schools and became discovered by the warmth that was Miss Herfa, an oasis beyond my mother's and my sister's skirts, language was a shame I could not bear to use, except when I was allowed to write it down. Speaking made people laugh at you, especially if you spoke too softly and hung your head so you could not be heard. Children mocked you, adults teased. Speaking opened your body to betrayal, speaking allowed you to be seen.

My mother said she and my father were afraid. I did not speak until I was two, they thought I was dumb. When I spoke, I spoke a whole sentence, 'Mamma, hear the thunder.' It was raining. But I remember speaking at home, to my mother and my father, and my big sister, who taught me everything she learnt in books before I was able to go to school. School was my experience of silence. For years I could not speak, silence was my snail's house on my back that kept me safe.

Had she too been unable to speak? Or was it that she spoke to the wrong man, like the people said, words in the twilight that he did not understand? Did her silence break, perforce? Did speech uncover her nakedness, once and for all, so that she had to cook cucumakka stick and throw away the baby? Where was the baby? In one of the graves between the naseberry trees, buried deep and dark in the earth's cocoon of silence? Did she go there when the peenie-wallies came out, to feed the dead?

Things started happening on the hill. At night there

were fires but in the morning the grass was not burnt. My Uncle Cuthbert, who told me all the stories I ever knew, said the sounds people said they heard was rolling calf quarrelling with three-foot horse, and somebody go dead. I had a deep and agonizing feeling of grief when I heard this. I had only ever lost one relative, my grandfather, whom I had not liked and whose death for me was only excitement and my first wake. But I thought the grief I felt that the woman who was strange and silent would die was like what I might feel if my mother died. I could not admit the thought of death side by side with the thought of my mother, so my mind veered away from that truth, and I refused to think about it any more.

I prayed to the image of Jesus that was in my mother's front hall, 'Do Jesus, don't make the noname lady die.' Jesus was somebody I could easily talk to, and had done from as far back as I can remember, because he too spoke in syllables of silence. I was never ashamed talking to him. He lived on an almanac on the boarding up of the hall, a half-man half-angel half-woman about whom I had unarticulated questions – like why was he an angel, which lived in heaven, and a man (he had a beard) and a woman (he had long hair) all at the same time. But it never seemed to matter because when I talked to him he seemed to understand. He understood without benefit of words, within the shadows of silence. I liked him very much. I thought there was something wrong with his heart because it showed through his chest and there was a writing saying, 'the bleeding heart of Jesus', but because he was always smiling, I thought he wasn't in any pain.

We started taking the long way around to meet my father in the bush, so we wouldn't have to pass the haunted house.

At night there were voices, people passing said, and

sometimes two figures instead of one flitting among the naseberry trees. One big tall black man in waterboots, khaki pants and a cambric shirt, they said. Serve her right, see it there now, she show off herself till she get so desperate, black man duppy come haunt her now. But you know, I hear long long time the man she use to along with is jus such a man, you know, big and strapping and good-looking with a shine black skin and always in him waterboots. Don't come from round here, come from somewhere up the line. Maybe St Elizabeth or Montego Bay or even Falmouth.

I didn't like the sound of that because the man they described sounded too much like my father. Once, only once, as in a dream, I saw my father speak to her. She asked him for a string of fresh fish he was carrying to the bushes to cook for lunch. Mostly he went on ahead of us in the early morning before the sun managed to finish drinking the dew water off the ground, and we followed him later, after we had done what we had to do in the yard to help our mother, and had had our porridge that would fill us up for the rest of the morning until my father cooked the lunch in a big kerosene tin over a bush fire at midday. This morning he was late because of getting the fish.

The string of fish was newly scaled and newly gutted and gleamed in the morning sun. She was a glimmer of my imagination silhouetted against the light which went through her dress, so that I thought I saw a ghost. Her hand was outstretched and when I came up panting behind my father, she had disappeared. I knew she had been there because he no longer had the fish.

When I asked him he said, 'She hungry and I give it to her. I don't want to hear you talking bout this.'

The morning was cool and fresh and still, a stillness

poised on an edge as if waiting for something to begin.

Our voices broke the silence.

I don't know if then is when the dreams begin, or is much later when my underground mind mature and start looping back, weaving stories back upon itself like a serpent's sinuous loop. I begin to feel as if I am drawn into a deep water, deep and dark under Morris Hole River where a navel string pass through my mother to my father and wrap round and round me and the noname lady in a deep bed of silence beneath the earth's core.

I screaming out in my sleep, 'Papa, Papa don't make her touch me! Papa don't make her touch me!' Snakes. Snakes. Snakes full up the water and it dark and thick like somebody throw away coffee tea dregs in the bottom, and I swimming towards the clear water choking up with scream and coffee tea water, swimming towards the clear water I can see under the twist-up mangrove root, but is a shadow standing between me and the clean water and is a man, a big, black grinning man with a snake between his legs with his hand claw like mangrove root twisted and black with his jawbone eat out like Grampa Eric jawbone the time he come to thief my brother Wycliffe and my mother had to grab Wycliffe and haul him out from the duppy hand.

I screaming bawling out for murder but the navel string between me and the noname lady heavy heavy pulling me back and the water fulling up my mouth with a river of silence, silence is an implosion in my chest that resists the surface, where breaking must be sound.

Snake man snake man move outa the way! Move move move outa the way!! Move your arse outa the way!!! Dark water swirls, rushes to a pinnacle, thunder bursts in my ears and the snake man with the tail between his legs reach out a

23

vast hand that grow and grow and grow and full up the world and lightning and thunder grow to a pinpoint of light and darkness roars out mightily as I break the surface into sound, 'Mamma! Papa!' And I wake in somebody's arms, too shaken and spent to guess who, wondering dimly in the underneath of my mind is which baby that wailing like it just born.

Rumour gave way to whispers. The noname lady had begun to swell. Every fourth Thursday when she come down to Miss Clemmy post office window to sign her register slip and give it back for a envelope with six England stamp and a blue register mark on the outside, people noticing things. First she covering not just her head but her whole body down to the hip with a big cloth like a shawl and she holding her face lower now. At first nobody guess why, they just think she getting more strange, but after a while it impossible to hide and whisper start to fly. 'You see it there now, duppy man breed her. Nothing in that belly there now you know, just wind and air. Is that happen all the time – you know how much woman go hospital with belly and can't deliver long after nine months because mitten inside? Doctor don't know what to do for this kinda thing bigger than doctor science.'

I was puzzled. Women only got that sort of thing when their husband die and somebody forget to plant the duppy or she forget to sleep in red panty so he can't come in the house. So the noname lady did married to the man that take her tongue then? When at peenie-wallie twilight she go out to feed the dead, is his dead duppy she go to feed and not a little baby drownded in cucumakka-stick tea?

See it there, is bad growth she have in her stomach. Cancer, her inside blue. Woman don't use up her inside, what you expect? Turn mule, belly can't find pickni to full it up, full up itself with something else. You see what I tell you?

But it wasn't duppy baby and it wasn't no cancer either.

One night a whole heap o' whispering and footfalling and bottle lamp flickering like giant peenie-wallie on the road below the hill by Miss Vie house and somebody send to call Miss Pertiss, the Maggotty and Mount Peace midwife from all the way in Retrieve. People say they hear rolling calf and three-foot horse and whooping boy and every kind of duppy noise you can think of wailing and running and bawling on the hill that night, and somebody hear like a graveyard singing, but the next morning when we wake up the news all over Baltree, Maggotty and Mount Peace, the noname lady have a little baby boy and nobody know is whose.

She call him Paul. Little after him born, she take off her head covering and start walk down to the Wesleyan church behind our house again, like people say she use to do before she turn strange. She take the baby with her, wrap up in a flowing white lace dress and bonnet and plenty white blanket like he going to a christening. In fact she did take him to christen, when he was about a year old. She herself wear either black or white, stark and plain against the sharp Sunday morning sun, and she always have on a hat that shade but not quite cover her face. I see her plain now and she long and maaga and her face long and maaga and straight, it don't look like anything in particular and it don't have no scars.

There was no ruin in her face.

She worship the little boy, even my mother who think her children is piece of sun and fly mustn't pitch pon we, thought so. She still don't talk to anybody more than so, but we notice how the little boy dress up like puss back foot, even in his yard, where the grass around the step was now cut and the step repaired. In addition to the every fourth Thursday envelope, sometimes in exchange for the register slip she get a parcel through the post office window. Parcel always mean clothes and other nice things from oversea, smelling nice the way people who come back from oversea always smell. We thought the little boy's endless supply of pretty clothes come in the parcel, shoes and socks even in the yard and sometimes when we passing the house where the windows sometimes open now even though no rocking chair still on the verandah, you hear her calling out to him, 'Paul, darling, careful now, don't take off you shoes and socks, makka wi juck you.' He was always taking off his shoes and socks, a small, fairskinned figure crouching down in the tall grass when we passed, lifting his head to stare at us with huge, preternaturally open eyes as shine as ackee seeds, but never speaking. Even when my bareface sister Magsie boldly said, 'Paul!' he never spoke, just continued staring unblinkingly while his little hands fumbled nervously at the confining socks and shoes. And, with an uncanny mother's sixth sense that her prize was in danger, she would come out quickly on the verandah and without looking at us, step down swiftly to scoop him in her arms and carry him inside the house, scolding so we could hear, 'Look at you now, don't I tell you not to put your bare feet in the dirt fore you catch jigger like those dirty nigger, and don't I tell you not to speak to dirty nigger pickni?'

She could speak. The discovery was devastating. I could not get over it. Her voice was neither strange nor mysterious, it was strong, slightly hoarse, and directed deliberately outward to and against us.

But the place where she raised it most was in church and afterwards on Sundays. Every Sunday in her black or white frock and the hat pulled down shadowing her face, she would sit in the parson mouth drinking in everything he say. But soon, in a hair's breath, she start to shout and carry on loud loud during the sermon, 'Hallelujah! Hallelujah! Thank you Jesus! Thank you Jesus!' disturbing the peace so is a wonder anybody else in church hear the sermon, and you know Wesleyan people is quiet people, just like Seven Day, don't make noise in church. After church going home she making up noise same way, all the long way on the road, shouting and shivering and weeping, 'Hallelujah! Hallelujah! Glory, Hallelujah, Jesus!' as if she have some great trouble that deeper than the depths of the sea, and no words on the face of the earth could reach but it pumping up with the fountain of her tears. What kind of trouble could she have now that the years of her barrenness was over, the good Lord smile on her and forgive her for the cucumakka-stick tea in which she drownded the baby, give her a second chance? What kind of trouble she could have now?

It was the child who was silent. In all the years I knew him, he never spoke.

Nobody knew who his father was. People speculated. People say is because she don't know who the father is, why she cry in church and return to her old noisy ways.

Some people say is a man from out the district that still come visit her by night. They waited expectantly but she never breed again and nobody don't see any man going or coming in her house. Some say is the Wesleyan parson but nobody could prove it, and the child don't look like him anyway. Some say is Long Man, who use to pass through our district like a ghost and stop at our house for a day or a week or two weeks, then disappear for another endless time on his errant journeys through the parishes in search of work that tied him down only long enough to find how to eat. Some

27

people, always ready for the complication of a mystery by a scandal, stretch credibility and say the child father is really the duppy that she feed, is whole heap of pickni don't too come right, when you check it out, don't the Bible tell you in those days there was giant in the land, because the sons of God see the daughters of men that they was fair, and come and have pickni with them? You don't see how the girl fair, almost white as sea salt. Who is to know if this sons of God them was not dead people who the Bible call sons of God because they gone on before? But some people say sons of God is fallen angel. See it there now, demon pickni. Demon have wife with the girl. The girl give demon wife. Is why the boy can't speak.

All this they said, but the boy was not yet two years old.

When he was two, my mother nearly went to jail for warning Luce Blagrove with a machete because Luce repeated in her hearing a rumour that the child was my father's. The whisper had been going round for some time and I was glad my mother warned Luce, though I was terrified she would go to jail and leave us for ever. But I was glad she warned Luce. I knew what Luce said wasn't true, because I had seen my father talk to the noname lady only once, that time he gave her the string of fish.

My father say Luce deserve a lick, she too facety and surance. I was sixteen when I left the district. The little boy was eight, and he still hadn't learnt to speak.

NATHAN

When he was only three years old, my brother Nathan showed up his true colours. Getting ready to get into his bed one night as if shop door close and business pack up as usual for the night, he just make a U-turn, walk over to my brother Tony, and poke him in the eye with his fingernail. With that, he climbed into bed, closed his eyes, and went matter-of-factly to his sleep. During all of this he uttered not a word.

His last act before poking his brother's eye was to kneel down by his bedside and say his prayers.

Before this incident, he never broke his bedtime ritual. And indeed, the movement from his knees to his feet and the slow turn round that take him 'cross the room to his brother's face was so smooth, so easy; if you didn't know better you would think it was part of the ritual self.

Tony start up one big self-righteous bawling and my father was going to haul Nathan out the bed to give an account of this, but when we explain to my father why, he just start to laugh, and my mother too. What happen was that earlier in the day Tony fight Nathan, take away his kite, run 'way with it saying he only borrowing it for few minutes, and then can't manage it, so he get it hook in a cucumakka tree and the whole kite tear up. Nathan didn't say a word, he just cut his eye and walk away. That was how he take his revenge.

That attitude of silent action is what characterize my brother all his life. He never speak much at any time, but especially not when he have a decision to make. He just make it, execute it, and that is that. No warning uttered, and if any questions asked, do your next best.

Between me and Nathan fell two years and Tony, who was younger than me by a year.

29

My brother was a man of dark blue silences. You thought of strong rivers, a striped blanket, furred and shadowed rock, the indifference of the sea. I knew silence as a different thing, a Joseph's coat of many colours. Mine was a silence of moons.

Except for a brief period during my teenage years when I knew the red heart of silence, as red as the heart of my brother's was blue. That was the time I fought my brothers as often as I could grab them unawares and kick, bite, scratch, claw in such ways that they could never fight back with anything approaching effectiveness. I hated boys with a passion whose only surcease was blood. All any of my brothers had to do was just brush against me if you think you bad, and I would kill them, then go to the river and scrub myself like there was no tomorrow.

I was making a washing for the dead.

No running water less than a river's deep flood, inexorably after the cleansing sea, could in those days rid me of the taint of boy. No domestic water could ever find in its stagnant stillness the drive and force to cleanse me of that dreadful stain: their dark hairy bodies, their breaking voices, their suddenly sproutings that invaded every space so that I could not turn, could not breathe, even, without bumping into an expanding grossness. For some reason which I never discovered, they hated me as much as I hated them, so they were as eager to fight me as I was to fight them. Because I was secretly afraid of as well as enormously repelled by these sprouting masculine bodies that like aliens had taken over my brothers' souls, I knew the only way to save myself from their dreadful menace was to attack first, and attack I did, as if surprise could somehow neutralize the terrible invasion. A secret I learnt early was that men can't really fight, not if you get them first. They fight by rules and standing off

30

and knocking fist to fist. I learnt to come from all direction, pinching and gouging and clawing, till their mind that always walk in a straight line get thoroughly confuse. I don't think I ever lose a fight with my brothers where I attack first, and for years I remembered this with pride, even after we reconcile into bigpeoplehood and I start taking interest in those same alien geographies that is called male.

During those years I fight with Nathan more than with my other two brothers. Because he use to be the closest, and I couldn't forgive him for becoming big, stupid and crass. I marvel now when I look back on those turbulent years, for my brother is actually a small man, as small for a man as I am for a woman, and so he could not have been that huge after all. But in those years, to me he was Hulk self taking up space nobody sell him.

◆

But in the beginning it was the two of us that were soulmates, welded together by our common need of silence. Silence was my snail's house on my back that I crawled in to escape the stare and ceremony of eyes. There I lived among the roots of things, holding conversation with ants which I discovered in every impossible hidden place, holding my face so close to the earth I could hear time grow. Inside my silent cocoons I looked out and saw real people like the shadows of trees walking.

My brother's need of silence was his need for an economy of existence that pared life down to its bone. Waste and spending was a thing he could not bear, all his life long. If bone could suffice, there was no need for flesh. My brother was as tight with words as he was with money, and with that he is the tightest man I ever knew. Even when we were children he use to keep a sweat-sleazy exercise book in which he record everything you borrow from him and every promise you make, every debt you owe him. Beside each, he write the date in his squeezed, tight handwriting like a grudgeful spider's explorations, and to the right of that the date of expected return or repayment, and to the right of that the date of actual return or repayment. The first category of debt – loans – was always meagre because my brother never lend anything except under great duress, such as blackmail, or, more seldom, the stress of affection he feel for me. The second and third categories was always fuller than the first, because promises made and debts owed could include such routine transactions as swopping chores for food, or secrets kept. We struggled and parleyed, like rituals of war.

'Cho, Nathan, don't be so mean.'

'You don't want me tell, two dumpling.'

'Boy, you mus dead bad. You going dead bad. Nutten can stop you from dead bad.'

No answer. Take it or leave it. You had no choice, you couldn't allow this to come to your parents' ears. You took it.

'Nathan, I hurrying, I late fi school. Wash the plates for me nuh?'

'Three piece of fish.'

'But that is Monday to Wednesday! You want I mustn't eat any meat? You want me dead from mirasmi?'

Silence. Take it or dead. 'How much one bulla equal?'

'Five mango.'

I really want the bulla cake, though at five East Indian mango the price too high.

'Awright, swop.'

My brother head nod. With words he was so parsimonious, rhythm sufficed.

Even before he go to school and could write for himself, my brother use to keep this exercise book. My mother perform the function of scribe, but not for things like secrets kept. Until he learnt to read, he kept that part of the reckoning in his head.

Today I speculate about the differences between our silence, my brother's and mine. Did the shock of some wave of prodigality, some encounter with my parents' legendary looseness with lucre, awaken in him the haunting fear of loss? Did the way possessions ran through my parents' hands strike terror into my brother's heart, force him into an early understanding of the rule of conservation? Or was it that their quarrels were so loud, so prodigal, that he sought by his own economy of verbs to contain what he might lose? For their quarrels haunted us with the fear that we would lose one, and therefore both. A man wounded in the bowels fruitlessly catches hold of his own intestines, holding them in against the force of their spilling. A child cries silently in the grip of a nightmare, hoping the will's resistance will arrest the tamarind switch, or make the marked skin not be marked after all.

But maybe we two were, again, just strange. My brother was asleep in the womb when he discovered his dark blue river of silence. Too young to have lost anything, or understood what it means to lose. My speculations are only the dishonesty of memory. I think these thoughts only because his silence lived with an urge to conserve possessions, mine with an urge to give them away. I am a creature of moons, I sideshift gazes. No one looks at another who is preoccupied with the things that are given. I give things so I do not have to give my spacer my silence, and that I may escape being seen. I do duties by you.

But in the beginning, all we were was just strange. My mother said we were her two largest babies and the two that worried her because for a long time we did not speak.

We liked the murmur of round water in the womb's round silence. Its soft icki tip icki tip icki tip like a clock under cloth or liquid in a small funnel falling.

We grew large and fat in there, not like other children who opened out to chatter and noises and the sun. We did not want to leave.

We were hard and easy births, my mother said, causing her more pain than she had thought possible, but coming quickly, soft and smooth, like slick fish, water children who loved the shadow of silence and had grown fat in it, who struggled between the urge to hold on tight, lock our small feet against extraction, and the pain we could not bear to give. We who were used to the round smooth shape of silence, without sharp edges. So we compromised, we became hard and also easy births.

We had a game that we played together, in our own secret language. A ritual was involved. We faced each other, standing at three feet's distance. Fixing each other's gaze, we marched to each other in a rhythmic line, forefinger extended in line with the nose bridge. When our noses were almost touching, we thrust our forefingers into each other's foreheads, chanting in perfect unison, '*Mana mana mana mahkita. Mana mana mana mahkita mana mana mana mahkita.*' The chant would increase in speed until the syllables tumbled over each other and our voices became a blur, even to our own ears, then rose to a crescendo and a triumphant flourish. '*Manamanamanamahkitamanamanamanamahkitama hkitamanamanamanaMAHKITA*!!!'

I have no memory what these syllables meant or where

we got them from, but we must have performed the ritual several times every day, and certainly every morning before we greeted the sun. We enjoyed ourselves enormously.

I remember that up to when I was six or seven, my sister had to bribe and threaten us to come play when she wanted to make up a foursome for skipping or play house.

We played either together or by ourselves. We dug earth silently side by side, searching for worms, which we then killed. Silently side by side we looped nooses in the spines of coconut leaves, which we called bone. We knelt silently over rocks and shrubs, still as only children can be still, and silently noosed unwary lizards who couldn't decipher our silence. These lizards we mercilessly hanged. Or my brother went off by himself to sit and think, and I went under the house to watch and talk with the ants. I rolled myself into a ball with my face as close to the ants' nests as I could get (so they could see me) and stuck my right index finger in my mouth and my left hand into my stomach, under my shirt.

I knew ants like silence, intimately. I knew the intricate twisted roads of their cities and I knew who were the soldiers and who cleaned the city, hauling grain after grain of tireless earth that fell into the gateways, banking each grain on middens outside the city's walls. Heaping them so neatly that the banked earth resembled new mincemeat falling from a shredder, or coconut after it falls in graceful loops from the grater onto the plate. Sometimes, to learn the city's belly's secrets, I carefully lifted off the top earth, the ants' roof of snail, so I could learn the marvellous rhizome of tunnels. The ants always got into a panic then, and quickly repaired the tunnel.

I knew ants like silence, intimately. I knew that if you stuck your finger in the path of a convoy, they would raise

35

an alarm, scatter in every imaginable direction, and make themselves a new trail. I knew who brought the food, and I knew their strength.

My brother understood my need to watch ants, and I understood his need to sit alone and watch the dark blue landscapes of his mind. I do not remember us talking, beyond *manamanamanamahkita*. I have clear memories of talk and feud with all my other siblings, but none with my brother, not when we were young, before the threshold of teens.

Memory which lies and weaves new truths with words, tells me we spoke without words. Memory hides the colour of forgetting. I have images of us suddenly falling apart in play, like two halves of an open fruit, he going to dream dark blue under the custard apple tree, I under the house after ants, without speaking. Our co-ordination as easy and as ripe as a fruit falling open, as round as the edgeless circle of silence.

My mother said we were strange. She said to the others, my sister when she pushed and thumped us for not playing, leave them alone.

I travelled to the city and entered a profession that fractured my silence. My brother became a farmer and looked out over the land with distant eyes.

But that was long after he had had many jobs and travelled to many places and then finally went back home.

My brother now has only one leg. The other he lost when he was working as a security guard in Savanna-la-Mar and showed up his colours to an irate motorist. I was abroad when it happened, and when I came back my sister Everette who goes to court every Tuesday and sometimes on Thursday just to hear testimony, for she loves sweetness but can't afford the shows at Roxy Cinema, told me what had happened.

She told it in a song that was all calypso, jazz and reggae

carnival, as my sister always tells, but this that I am singing is a song of silences, the music syncopates, attenuates, fifes itself beneath the earth. This that I am singing is a song of fifes. So I must translate my sister's song.

The man come up to my brother and say 'Open the gate.'

My brother say, 'Show you ID.'

'Open the gate.'

'Show you ID.'

'Open the blasted gate. You know who me is?'

My brother had done with speaking. It was his way.

My brother point to the sign above the gate: 'No entry without a valid Hotel Rosseau ID. All visitors use the gate at the next turning up the road left.'

'That is for visitor. I is not no visitor. You know who I is?'

Silence.

'I is the blasted MP for the area. But is where they get this stupid likkle ass country boy eh? Everybody round here no know me?'

Silence.

'Boy you don't know you own MP?'

Silence. Silence.

'But I shouldn't surprise. You mus be a bloody Labourite, fool like backside.'

My brother was a diehard PNP.

The motorist haul his other foot from where it hanging in the car door and try to push open the gate.

My brother push the gate back, and haul a big concrete and steel he keep for the purpose across the road. The car can't move.

The man chuck my brother, my brother chuck him back.

My brother have a gun, a security guard gun, but he never use it. When the man chuck him again he cuff the man one rahtid cuff in his face nearly take the head off the neck how it twist round like a gig.

By this time crowd gather and a gun go off. The man say is a accident, he never mean to shoot. But my brother foot splinter to the bone and they had to take it off. My brother who never had any need of flesh, if bone could suffice.

The court case take three years and my brother get a new leg, not bone, plastic, and he get five hundred and sixty thousand dollars which he put in the bank and go back to farming.

◆

My brother is now married, with three children. His wife is a noisy woman who bangs pots and pans loudly against surfaces, and hollers for the children at the top of her lungs, 'Shanique! Olivene! Hosein! Find youself right here this minute fore I come fi you!' as if to drown out the sound of silence. My brother thinks the sun shines from the ground she walks on. He still does not talk much, even to her, but when you see them together, you know he is a happy man.

I pass through once in a blue while, haunting the old places in search of silences I have lost. Our meetings have of themselves taken the form of other rituals, though I don't know if he realizes. Certainly I didn't, until I came to write this song. Always we sit together out in the yard on the bamboo bench, side by side, he with his head bent, hands clasped between his thigh and the softly swinging man-made leg, and the sun shining in his hair so you can see the cocoa-brown scalp where the hair is cut low. Mostly we do not speak.

Occasionally I murmur a syllable or two, an idle comment on how so little, or so much, has changed, a question about whether the planting is going OK. He nods seriously from time to time in answer to my question. But mostly we just sitting, not talking. Just sitting in silence.

She is inside banging pots and singing 'Nearer My God to Thee' in a massive contralto that makes the funeral hymn sound like resurrection cymbals, full of morning. She comes out in the yard, a big, warm-fleshed woman taller than her husband, wearing no more than a light shift through which her massive breasts are exposed. Because of the heat, she says. Her flesh spills over actual space. Lush, imperious, it soaks up and rounds out light like blotting paper. It would be easy to say she is a big, blowsy, crude woman vulgarly unclad, her unconscious nakedness an offence. But it would depend on which angle you are standing at in relation to the light. Here, the sun has escaped into her presence and you are instead conscious of warmth and fierce energy, an abandoned prodigality of being that is at once exhausting and welcoming. Particles of energy like motes of dust on sunlight rush, swirl, eagerly towards her, she draws them in. And flings them out. She draws energy and radiates it, takes and gives it back, gives it and takes back. Gives it again. She is like a constant wave of the sea, not a river. No, not rivers, this woman, not rivers with their runes and dark murmurous secrets.

She carries a large pudding pan full of dishes under her arm. She goes to the outside concrete stand on which she piles the washed crockery so that it can dry catching the sun. It will dry smelling warm and sun-kissed.

'Nearer my God to Thee! Nearer to Thee!
'E'en though it be a cross

39

'That raiseth me! Shanique! Olivene! Hosein!

'Bring you backside come here now, you hear me?'

She passes by her husband, cuffs him carelessly and affectionately across the back of the head, and continues on into the house, singing and shouting in blinding syncopation. Both her songs are punctuated by new bangings as she tackles the tidying of the house. Trails of light, some virtue of the sun, seem to go into the house with her.

I am not tempted to wonder how my brother can be happy in the midst of so much noise. I myself, in another life, married a man of silences, whose silence was all sharp edges, cutting all people out. The river child, who had loved the round silence of the womb and given her mother a hard and easy birth, heaved her own womb and spat him out. Went away bleeding. In search of silence.

My brother is still the tightest man I ever knew, but not as tight as he used to be. Now he has stretched like elastic that has been worn.

THE IDIOT

My mother said the thing you despise is the thing that will come back to haunt you. She always had a stack of proverbs to remind you of this: 'Ole ooman no done climb no throw 'way you stick … never know the use of half a knife till it lost … the stone the builder refuse is become the head of the corner.'

She told us stories, too, not real stories like my Uncle Cuthbert who told me all the real stories I ever knew, but stories about herself, her childhood and her father and growing up. One story was about how she malice a man name Pa Brown who did faas with her, and one day she had was to depend on him to carry her cross a raging river.

'Ah pass him by the road an Ah hol me head straight, for I determine I not talking to him. But the whole time Ah wondering how Ah going cross to the other side for the river come over and even if you can swim is serious danger you putting youself in, and I couldn't swim.'

My mother say she look down on the raging brown water and she see her death. But she pray Puppa Jesus help me now, with the malice in her heart and she not looking at Pa Brown who coming along behind her and she can feel him smiling behind her back like, 'Watch here now, what this woman go do, ehn?'

She make two step fi go in the water but it really swift and deep and she don't think her foot can stand the strain, for she wasn't a big woman, no ballast inside her frame.

Well, Pa Brown just come up longside her and say, 'You want me take you over?' My mother so shame, she jus look 'way and say 'tenky'. I could just imagine my mother face and her neck when she say that, she have a way of throwing up her head proud proud like her ancestor was chief in Africa, and screw up her mouth like she bite down on lime or suck bitter orange, and is she is the queen and you feel like is you is the beggar and she really doing you a favour.

Pa Brown stoop down and my mother get on his back and is so he take her across, a big strong strapping man in water boots and using his cutlass for strong hold and balance in the water. He put her down on the other side and tip him beat-up beat-up felt hat to her and walk 'way, not a word said. After that whenever he see her he nod his head and tilt the beat-up beat-up felt hat with the rat holes in the crown but he never say a word, and she just nod back and say, 'Good evening, Sir' or 'Good morning, Sir', in her most dignify courthouse voice, her head fling up like queen and her mouth purse up like suck orange and she giving out largesse. But inside she well shame. And when his wife die, my mother who don't follow up wake for is only hootiah and heathen go to such place, she go both the funeral and the wake. And I swear I sure the only thing she say to him at that funeral and that wake is, 'Good evening, Sir', and he nod and tilt the beat-up hat in her direction.

My mother, who wasn't humble, told us this story frequently to teach us how to be humble, and for years that story haunted me because of Ezekiel Watkiss. One time I even had nightmares thinking my punishment might be not to be carried across water but to be married to him for my sins.

Ezekiel was in my class when I was eight years old and my mother had decided to move me from Miss Nelson's school in Maggotty where I wasn't learning as I should because I was scared of the strap, and send me instead to Miss Herfa and Man Teacher school next door in Black Shop. Ezekiel turned

42

up to school only sometimes, but he was bright, really bright, and it showed, especially on Thursdays.

Thursdays were my favourite because that was when we had recitation and vocabulary and spell and take down, one whole bright afternoon handling the sound and feel and texture of words in your mouth. Some smooth as silken sweets lolling on your tongue, Othere the old sea captain who dwelt in Heligoland, Torfrida ran and ran and ran. Others rough and raised and risky like the tops of mountains and hills, dry clashed his harness in the icy caves and barren chasms. Some singing like songs, southward, northward, visible, invisible, see the kind baker in cap clean and white, busily baking from morning till night, half a poun a fipinny rice half a poun a weevil. Others sharp and secret and ready to pounce, lurking in bushes and unexpected over smooth ground, like snake and swish and seacat and schemes and scheming.

Long bright afternoons which were the only times we got to go outside under the big guango tree in the school yard where it was always cool, no matter how hot the day. If I stood on tiptoe on the hump in the ground up by where the fowl coop for the school farm project was, I could see out towards Lucea by the sea where the breezes came off to cool us down on these hot Thursdays during the spell and take down.

We stood in a line and Miss Celine was always having to call to us because the line was never quite straight, we were always wriggling like eels in a bamboo gourd, and she would call out the words in order of how we were standing. If you couldn't spell your word when it got to your turn, you would have to go to the back of the line. The next person who couldn't spell a word would go behind you, and so on and so on until everyone had had a turn, and the person

43

at the head of the line was declared the winner. Then we would start all over again. I liked spell and take down only halfway because although I usually got to go to the top of the line, I used to feel real bad for the boys in the class. They always got sent either to the back of the line, or if they were really hopeless, to the fowl coop to feed the chickens and sometimes to tie out Man Teacher goats. The boys didn't come to school much, not more than so, and when they come, if they come on a Thursday, they end up at the back of the line. The duncest girl in the class could always not feel so bad because the person at the back was bound to be a boy.

'Bas,' Miss Celine would say in her deep deep voice like the Wesleyan church organ playing behind our house in Pan Land, so that I could not get tired of listening to her, 'spell Mississippi.' Bas was a long roughbone boy who always wearing short khaki pants that shorter and tighter than him. For years he was in Third Class where the average age was thirteen, and must have been at least seventeen. And he only move up to there because Man Teacher wife, Miss Herfa, thought it look bad to keep him in First Class among all the little children, plus he was good with the animals and that counted for something. When Miss Celine tell him to spell Mississippi or some hard word like that (though every word was hard for Bas), Bas just hang his head with a foolish look on his face and shuffle his mansize big toe in the dust of the school yard, and a few of the girls start to giggle. I use to hang my head down too and hold my breath tight tight tight waiting for Bas release. But Miss Celine always let a good full minute pass like is silence for the dead before she say, 'Go feed the goats, Bas', and Bas just stumble off and disappear in sheer relief and I let out my breath with a soft 'phhh' hoping nobody hear. He would stay disappear until next time his father allow him time off from helping him on his land, and then he would turn up in school again for another one, two, three days and go either to the goat pen or the back of the line.

I use to wonder why boys like Bas didn't just stay away on Thursdays rather than going through all the shame before the whole class out in the school yard. But my mother said those boys skin thick like alligator, for they use to it, and furthermore they have company for is most of them in that situation. None of them can spell so who go laugh?

'But the girls laugh, Mamma.'

'That is nothing. That don't bother them. But if boy laugh now, that is where the attaclaps come in.'

It was a sort of ritual we all knew by heart. 'Bas. Spell coconut.' Pause. Minute of silence. 'Bas. Go feed the goats, Bas.' And Bas shambling off into the tall grass, the sun shining in his eyes and he throwing up his arm at the last minute to shield his face from the glare that make your eyes water.

The only boys who could spell were Ezekiel Watkiss and Wellesley Black. They called Wellesley Goggleye because of his eyes which bulged like those of a goggleye, a fish with eyes that seemed to come out on stalks that next to kingfish and snapper was a special dish you could afford only on Sundays. Wellesley came to school regular and he was really bright. His sister Nerissa was a pupil teacher but mostly she didn't teach us, she taught the lower grades. Wellesley was the right age for Third Class. I wasn't because I had skipped several grades, and Wellesley didn't like that at all. Spell and take down and end-of-year exams were really tense business because everyone knew it was going to be between me and Wellesley for first place, since Ezekiel not regular in school, and in the exams often only half a point separate the first- and second-place winners. At the end of the Third Class year Wellesley and me tied for first place because I couldn't understand bauxite (why Miss Celine cursing bad word?), and where in the exam they ask, 'What do we get from bauxite?' I write, 'yam, potato and dasheen'. Miss Celine had drilled us every day for weeks and she was really upset. She told everybody, including Miss Herfa, who found it funny and laughed till I wanted to drop down and die, for Miss Herfa was my idol and I lived by every word that proceeded out of her mouth like God.

I beat Wellesley at spell and take down ten times out of ten. But it was not so easy to beat Ezekiel Watkiss, who, like Bas, came to school in a blue moon. But all his sisters – there must have been at least ten of them, they were so many – came regularly. His big sister Bathsheba was also a pupil teacher.

Ezekiel's nickname was Hog. He was a really ugly boy, people said, with grained skin the colour of burnt ashes. The children teased him a lot, but what I remember about him was that he never answered, he always had this soft, reasonable kind of way that even then I found strange, it just never make any sense to me. On the road going home in the evenings when the others shout 'Hog!' trailing behind him and arcing small stones like accidents so they would fall against his bare heel like nobody fling them there, he would turn round and say things like, 'Don't say that, you mustn't say that', or, 'You think it is right to call people hog?' as if he really expect them to answer, 'Awright Ezekiel' or, 'No, Ezekiel' in a quite reasonable way. He have a soft careful kind of voice like when hot potato in somebody mouth and they fraid to bite down on it, is so he fraid to bite down on his consonants. At first sometimes when he say these things the children would be so shock, they just fritter into silence, but mostly after the first shock they get seriously vex, and is pure stone-throwing and chanting, 'Ezekiel Watkiss, yu mout favour hog! Hog! Hog! Hog!' Mostly though I think they fraid of what their parents would do or maybe of what this mysterious boy would do for they always fling carefully so the stone don't touch him on purpose, but the whole crowd follow behind him till he take the turning that lead over the hill to where he live at Mango Walk.

I often wondered how he had such a nice sounding name, all smooth and dancey and stately like Othere and Daniel and Gideon and Deerslayer and living in Heligoland, and then a nickname such as Hog. I wondered if maybe his father or his mother was a poet because they all had these really beautiful names, like someone had thought of singing: Rebecca and Bathsheba and Winsome and Carmelita and Gabriel and Curtley and the youngest, Grace Annabella.

The Watkiss family was known for many reasons. Their father, Jeremiah Watkiss, was always working but they seemed to remain poorer than the rest of us. My mother said it was a curse, somebody in the family from way back must be did do something and now the sins of the fathers is visited on the children even unto the third and fourth generation, is so retribution go, don't make duppy fool you. It was very strange to me because all of them went regularly to church, but is the jump-up Pocomania church they go to and in my mother book that was another part of the problem.

They were the only family that lived in a house with a dirt floor. In our district that was a serious kind of disgrace, like lice or slavery or yaws, which people spoke about in whispers or in cursings but which you never saw, so you knew those things were from way back, donkey's years before anybody in the world was born. My mother use to say things like, 'I don't want you mixing up with those Murphys for nothing name Murphy not good. They have yaws. Is a bad breed.' I had never seen yaws and it didn't occur to me to ask my mother what it was because I knew it must be something dreadful, something so utterly unmentionable that if you discussed it you were bound to get it. We and the Murphys were distant cousins, too distant for us to get yaws, for we never got it.

I never saw inside the Watkisses' house because my mother didn't allow us to go to other people's house since there were nine of us and your brothers and sisters are more than enough company so what more do you want, whatsoever cometh of more than these is evil, keep you foot in you house, you hear. But I pass by it several times coming from watching cricket at the Oval at Mango Walk. It wasn't a real oval, just a cleared space of ground where the men went to play on Sunday afternoons, carefully dressed in their pressed whites with sharp four seam, and we children sometimes went along too, if our father was playing and he was in a good mood. Mostly he wouldn't allow the girls, just my three brothers, because he said gal pickni not suppose to be roaming up and down on road like hootiah. But sometimes, because I was his favourite, I could get things from him, so my bigger sister Magsie would send me to beg for the rest of us.

It was strange, but in the same way that Ezekiel's sister being a pupil teacher never stopped the children from teasing him mercilessly, what we knew about their family never let the children tease or be rude to Bathsheba. I think it was more than just the terror of Miss Herfa's strap or of Man Teacher, whom we all feared. I think it was because they were afraid, full stop. Because of Bathsheba.

Bathsheba was tall and stately with skin like the underside

of a cocoa leaf, and she was so quiet, you felt you could reach out and touch her quietness, only you felt it would have been liberty-taking – you felt prohibited, somehow. It wasn't that she was silent, because she wasn't – she taught, and she spoke plenty in the class, just as much as the other teachers. But she had this untouchable space around her, as if she wrap herself in quiet like a cloak, only it was not outside but deep deep inside her, not something of her own effort at all but just the way Bathsheba was. The year I was eight one of my favourite books which I was allowed to raid from Man Teacher office shelf was *Lorna Doone* by R. D. Blackmore, and I always thought of Bathsheba when I read *Lorna Doone*. Don't ask me why. No illogic struck me because I didn't know *Lorna Doone* was white people and we were black people. The pictures in the books I read were pretty people. Up to that time I had never seen a white person. White people was something like yaws, or mad, or obeah, or consumption in your family, that is, distant and terribly strange, only in a niceish way. (Except for the ones in Rhodesia, who my mother told me about, holding black people captive.) So I didn't really think of Bathsheba and *Lorna Doone* like white people or black people, or work out why it was I thought of her the way I did. It was more a quality, a nuance, a shadow, a shiver of signs, some trace that rippled somewhere on the edge of your mind that you couldn't call a name but it was there. Bathsheba was all of that and she and *Lorna Doone* were well mix up in my mind. She was mixed up too in my dreams with the Morris Hole River where my mother who was an Adventist washed her clothes early on Sunday mornings and my grandmother Gertrude on my father side and my great-grandmother Sister Sis on my mother side washed babies in silence when the fog just coming up before the sun rise, both still washing the baby although they dead long time and one dead in Maggotty five miles away, up where the river head begin.

We were all a little afraid of Bathsheba. She was very beautiful. I wondered if she was a rivermumma, or a changeling like in *Grimm's Fairy Tales* and the *Yellow, Blue* and *Red Fairy Books.* Yet she was nice. She didn't beat and she spoke in a soft, cushiony voice like her brother. But she was never really there. I don't know how else to explain it.

But her elsewhereness was enough. Nobody teased Ezekiel when she was there, and I think he didn't say anything to her about what happen on the road going home after school, for she never said anything to any of us.

The following year I went to high school along with the five other girls who had passed either Common Entrance or Grade Nine Achievement, and I didn't see Ezekiel much because when I was coming home from school he was either at school still or at work with his father, and my mother didn't allow us on the road after school like hootiah. But when I was in Fourth Form he took the Grade Nine Achievement and passed and came to our school wearing green khaki with starch when everyone else was wearing brown khaki and starch had gone out of style because it was wash and wear that was all the rage. He stuck out a mile and everyone laughed of course.

Ezekiel began to engross my thoughts because of what now happened on the road going home from school in the evenings. We all got on the same bus from Lucea to Maggotty and got off the same bus to walk the mile and a half to our district, because it was only the one bus and if you missed it your corner dark, you would have to walk the whole nine miles and plus home. Nobody except me spoke to him. The other girls pointedly ignored him and behind his back they explained why. 'Him too eggs up, him and we is not fren, and if him think just because him coming to high school now we go talk to him, him have another think coming. In him green khaki suit!'

It was easy for Ezekiel to talk to me because I always fell behind, reading library book or cocooning silence. He use to trail behind to fall in step with me and that was another ritual: I never said anything, making a great show of being absorbed in my book, and he would just sort of scuff along, head down, looking like somebody searching for something to say. Silence bobbed and weaved and stumbled uneasily between us, like a skein of crochet that miss the right stitch way up top, and have to unravel and begin again. I wishing he would change his mind and hurry up and go because I shame to be seen in his company, I don't want anybody laughing at me for talking to an obvious country boy in green khaki when everybody know is brown wash and wear you must wear, and I don't want anybody carrying news to my father that I talking to boy of any sort or kind – is that your poor parents sacrifice and send you to school for? Worse, I don't want him to think I like him for I don't like no boy, and even if I choosing boy to like is not this one with the face that everybody call hog. But deep down I shame the most because I can find no good reason not to talk to this boy who so nice I really want to hate him, but I feel he might get uppity and think we is quabs, and I vex with myself for all these things and for daring to feel sorry for him as if he lesser than me. Something in me shame for that worst of all, but still I sorry for him even though I feel I have no right. Something curl up and knot up like the crochet thread in my stomach for some whisper on the edge of noise tell me this boy bigger than me. I feel physically bad. But still I not backing down.

51

But he break the purling silence, and he always start out soft and hesitant, testing words in his fraid-of-consonant mouth same as how a man feel the quality of a stone's smoothness in his palm, rolling it between finger and thumb, before he put it in the catapult and shoot. Silly things like, 'So Marlene, how is school?' or, 'What is your favourite subject? I bet is English', as if him is some parent or older person making conversation with schoolchildren. That comparison made me even more determined to protect myself. I always answered him in carefully chosen monosyllables in my best English, careful as my mother in her best courthouse voice, my head fling up like queen and my mouth purse up like suck orange and I giving out largesse. And the syllables were part of an interrupted conversation, as I went to pains to let him know, ducking my head back into my book with the purposefulness that showed you thought somebody had spoken without saying 'Excuse' – no manners at all.

His patience belonged in a world below necessity which I could not understand. You couldn't yell 'Corn!' 'Soup!' or 'Cheap histrionics!' – any of the fad phrases or big words you tested out on each other in class every day. There was no room in Ezekiel's presence for humour or slyness. His patience and sorrowfulness seemed to come from a long way away, from places whose outer shapes were secret behind his eyes, their close interiors a stillness that stayed while the earth spun. I was angry and troubled beyond anything I could explain. I remember only snatches, bones and rags of speaking.

One day he said, 'Why you don't want to talk to me? What I do?' and I answered inside my own head, 'Why you pick on me? Why you don't go ask the others that question? Why is always me you want to talk to?' Out loud I said, the lie a deliberate insult, my voice clipped and scissoring like my mother the queen in court, 'I don't have any problem talking to you. I talking to you now, don't I?'

The old Ezekiel, the boy who said the most unreasonable things in a reasonable voice as if he expected people to agree with him, surfaced, as exact as water rising or buried bone. 'I am not less than you, you know, Marlene,' he said. Not, 'You think you better than me?' so I could trace him, tell him where to get off, but, 'I am not less than you, you know, Marlene', as if him is Sabbath School teacher wooing dearly beloved children to principle and promise and there is no joke here.

If I could have detected hypocrisy or self-righteousness in him, I could have borne it. I could have forgotten both him and my own sense of sin. But in the same way I had only metaphors for his sister, I had no way to read him. He was a palimpsest obscured by signs. With every word I thought, he slipped further away from sight. But always he left stains, enigmatic bright and fading crimson I tried both to press – so I could see the colour clearly – and to rub out against the shadow of white cloth.

It is strange, but you can actually live in a district with someone and not see them at all, or once in a blue moon, or you see them somewhere else. My last remembered sight of Ezekiel Watkiss was of him standing on the steps of the main school building looking down on girls talking about him in deliberately loud and cruel voices, the week before he dropped out of school. I am sure I must have seen him many times afterwards, but this is what I remember.

The following year I took my O levels and moved to St James and another school for A levels though I wanted to go and work, but my mother said at fifteen I was too young and she didn't want any old hootiah in necktie harassing me before I was old enough to defend myself.

I hear Ezekiel became a big contractor and heading up a well-known company that make fancy town houses in St Andrew. I could have breathed easy if the old childish fear had remained, because I heard he also married and became the father of children. Bathsheba and most of his sisters, like most of the rest of us, left the district, either for abroad or the city. I wonder if he now lives in one of the biggest houses in town, a house with top of the line terrazzo tiles and a shining portico and a paved walkway so your feet don't touch the ground, and what he would say if he knew I haven't even arrived at the place where I am paying a mortgage.

Or maybe the years and success haven't changed him at all and he is still impossibly whole.

That, I know, is impossible. But Ezekiel Watkiss, Hog, was always impossible.

Sometimes I finger and fiddle the idea of picking up the telephone and saying hi. He's only a telephone call away, the number is listed in the directory. But what would I say?

The thought of what I could not say keeps the telephone on its cradle.

Memory and moment are never the same. The one can be recreated, reinvented, even made to become whole. The other never returns, and when it comes, too often glimpsed as other than itself. Falling in the spaces between knowing and not knowing, between silence and not speaking.

I would have liked to remember myself as tall and brave and heroic and different, like the children they write about in books and show in movies nowadays, defying death and shame and public opinion to make one last stand in the cause of a friend, or someone perceived as friend.

But the truth is far less shining, and far more stained.

He still scatters himself every now and then across my dreams. As my mother's stories. Which are not real stories but stories about herself, her childhood and growing up.

MISS MINNIE

He often wondered who his real mother was. But he felt no curiosity to meet her or see what she was like in the flesh. The woman who had cared for him from a toddler, as far back as he had sense enough to understand, was everything he felt and understood of the word.

His father said his mother was dead, and that was the end of that. But the people in the district said differently. They said she had danced go-go in a nightclub and after he was born she grew restless for the old free ways and so she picked up and left. One bright morning she just laid him in the bed and tell Miss Florrie she just going out to the shop, she soon come back. But she never come back and is Miss Florrie hear the baby crying after dark and realize he all alone and wet in the house. They said his father never mentioned her name again and if anyone else ever did he get dark. He knew it was true for in all the years he never heard from his father's lips his mother's name, and though he would have liked to talk about her, instinct told him he wasn't to ask.

After his mother 'died', his father went out and got this woman, Miss Minnie, from way up in St Ann, as if he prefer distance and silence between him and his wife antecedents, and he marry her and bring her to look after his infant son.

Miss Minnie was sufficient. She fed and crooned and sang to him and helped him take his first steps, and when it was time for school she held his hand and carried him the first day. Miss Minnie had no children of her own. It was her cross to carry, the people said, singing in church in low crooning voices, and she bear it with such humility and patience. The little boy was the apple of her eye. Not a thing that she don't take a interest in, and if him go outa street, fly can't brush on him.

She was a small thin woman with a sharp tongue and a restless way of moving her head as if perpetually dissatisfied, looking around her for something that should come but was too long a time in coming. She made quick darting movements like a lizard and had her hair in bright tie-heads where the colour never seemed to diminish, and she worked hard in the fields with his father, carrying the reaped produce long distances on her head in a ground basket to Lucea market where she sold yams and vegetables to extend the income from what his father earned repairing shoes.

She always brought back something for him in her apron pocket, deep earth-stained folds of cloth in which he had to dig deep to find the striped candy walking stick or the grater cake or ginger drops buried there. Sometimes if it was holiday time from school he went with her to the market, riding between the hampers on the donkey which carried the part of the produce that wasn't on her head. Sometimes, on days when business was slow, his father shut up the shop and went too, but mostly he had to divide his energies between the shop and the fields.

She didn't talk a lot but she observed everything: she noticed even new blades of grass shooting between one morning and the night before. When she spoke it was short and sharp and to the point. She wasn't a woman much given to affection: her way was to see that he was scrubbed clean and well fed, went regularly to school and had all the books and other things he needed. And the striped candy or grater cake or drops in the apron pocket. She didn't touch him caressingly after he started going to school, and as he grew older she moved physically further and further away from him.

The father didn't talk at all. So Miss Minnie suited him fine. He liked the sound of his own self surrounding him, under and above the steady beat of the hammer on the last where he sat in the shop pounding shoes. If the boy spent any time in his presence, it was to sit quiet as a mouse on a stool in the shop's shadowed corner, watching with big solemn eyes the rhythmic rise and fall of the hammer on the last, or his father's deft, sinewed hands as he handled the leather with rare delicacy, tender as a lover as he felt the grain for texture and softness and wear. Sometimes he would grunt out an instruction or two in a gruff undertone, which seemed to come out of the underside between his neck and his chin, but the boy understood. He rose with quick, delicate, darting movements oddly like Miss Minnie's, to perform whatever task his father had called him to, handing a nail here, a pot of glue there, a strip of cast-off leather from the pile in the corner, then resumed his grave-eyed vigil on the stool in the shop's shadowed corner, himself a shadow among its shadows.

Sometimes people coming in didn't see him at all, he kept so quiet, and is only when the men start getting too boisterous with the talk and start telling unclean jokes and coded stories about women they liked or had had, that his father would clear his throat warningly and someone would look over in the corner and say, 'But Jesus Christ, I never see the boy there at all. Boy, you is duppy or what, how you so quiet?' and maybe cuff him affectionately over the head with a curled palm.

He loved being in the shop when the men came in, ostensibly to do business but mostly to exchange the day's gossip and listen to Maas Baada read the one newspaper aloud so everybody could hear, those that could read and those that couldn't. Maas Baada used to say, 'Boy, when you get bigger and start go high school is your turn, you wi haffi read for the man dem because by that time my eye get old and dark, young blood haffi take over.' He felt pleased at the thought of being the one to take over the reading, the voice that would keep the men together and keep them coming to the shop. Vaguely he wished his father would talk to him more, or even cuff him over the head with a curled palm the way Maas Baada and others of the men did. But he told himself Miss Minnie was sufficient.

When he was ten he went to the high school in Lucea and made acquaintances but no real friends. Miss Minnie came to all the Parent-Teacher meetings and gave meticulously whatever was required of her, her labour on fund-raising days, her hardwon pennies wrung from the stubborn earth in years of drought when the school said parents had to contribute to this and that for times were hard. When he was fifteen his father died, as silently as he had lived, lying down in his bed one morning and sleeping off instead of rising early to go to the field before opening the shop as he used to do. The autopsy said he had suffered a heart attack. Everybody was surprised for he was a thin strong man who had never had a day of illness that anyone could remember, but the doctor said he died of a diseased heart. A heart which was diseased and lay silent, quiet as water under stone, then just suddenly up and attacked him. People said Miss Minnie missed nothing for he had never loved her, all his heart was on that go-go girl that give him the one son and then up and left him braps.

There was a wake and a funeral and then it was he and Miss Minnie alone. He offered to leave school and go to work but Miss Minnie said, short and sharp, 'Over my dead body.' But later that night she came into his room and said, 'Boy, I don't want you to think I ungrateful or anything, but I want you to know you not to fret about me, I can manage. What I want is for you to finish what your father wanted, go to school and finish you education and get a good job so you can hol up your head in this district and one day get to leave and go somewhere where you can prosper, for this is a place that hol you down and it have plenty bad-mind people here that don't want to see you progress. If you want to help me, just study your book.' It was the longest speech she had ever made and she never made another.

Over the next two years he worked as hard as he could in school, and watched her working her hands to bone to send him regularly and with books in his bag and food in his stomach. The house fell into disrepair and Miss Minnie got thinner and stringier and more like a lizard in her movements, quick and nervous now not like she waiting for something to come but more like she trembling for fear it will not come. When he was seventeen he won the Jamaica Scholarship and went to the university where he studied Economics. He graduated and got a good job with a multinational firm in the city. He took an apartment there in the city and drove a company car, and he sent for Miss Minnie to come live with him for he was afraid for her loneliness there in the country and she working herself to the bone.

She refused, feeling she was imposing on him and blighting his prospect when he was so young, scarcely fending for himself. But he insisted, telling her he needed her to keep house for him, for he really couldn't manage by himself with a workday that sometimes went up to ten o'clock at night. And so he sought to save her pride.

Eventually she gave in, doubtful, but glad to do

whatever she could for him. She kept the place speckless and shining, all days and mornings earlier than the sun rising to buff this piece of furniture or that piece of kitchen counter with her beeswax and a piece of soft cloth that she take from the country for she don't trust town polish, too hurry come up and watery and artificial. Days and mornings all hours cleaning and washing and tidying, going over and over lost specks that had missed her cloth and soap and polish on the first going-over, carefully husbanding her love in the small steadily shrinking spaces between one cleaning and another. For the truth was the apartment was small and sheltered from dust by its air-conditioned upstairs enclosement and there was very little for her to do. There was a washing machine but she never used it, she went to the outside downstairs sink to wash, for she said whoever hear bout machine washing clothes, machine have hand and foot, machine know which clothes not to put in because they run, or how to sort the whites from the coloureds? And what about when you want to blue the clothes to make them white? Furthermore no machine not running she, she is smaddy and machine is machine, who in charge? She grumbled these things to herself as she worked, more voluble now than she had been in the past.

But only to herself. She grumbled to keep herself company as she pieced out the work to make it last. To keep herself sane and to disguise from him that she knew he had only asked her because he was sorry for her, that she knew there was no real work here. She sought to save his pride, even as he had sought to save hers.

She grumbled to herself but she made herself silent and small if he brought guests home, especially if he brought a girl. She would seem, but it was an illusion only, to curl herself into a ball in the corner of conversations, seeking to erase herself from the gaze of eyes to which he had introduced her, deferring to his desire for her to be there rather than hiding off in her own small room, but holding herself tight as a snail in a shell, evading the eyes. After several unsuccessful attempts by his guests to draw her jovially into conversation 'What happening Mummy? How you so quiet? Miss Minnie how the country? You know I always wanted to live in the country, for this town life really get on you nerves, you turn into a artificial person, you lose every sense of what is real ... so Miss Minnie I hear you is a big farmer, you plant pawpaw and them things there? Boy, is my kinda food those man ... Ah really have to come visit you one day you know', as if she going back home and the day set already – after several attempts like these, he stopped bringing people home.

She saw and became quickly distressed. She was shadowing away in the close closed apartment with windows which you had to lock at night and open by day, and when you opened them you looked down on the faces of streets the roofs of cars and the loss of inner space. She flitted about as a shadow among shadows, her movements now no longer those of a small reptile of the bush, but careful, carved, seeking to fit themselves into the space of an ill-imagined cage. He saw and became quickly distressed.

On the morning when she made up her mind to speak to him about the situation, to let him know she was going back to the country where she belonged, among trees and leaves and the falling welcome of her own house's fading rooms, a woman came to the house.

Miss Minnie was in the outside downstairs wash area wiping the tiles with Ajax cleanser and trying to contain the ache of her arthritis beneath the mask of a smooth face which she now habitually wore even in her own company alone, as if she herself was a mirror looking through secrets she didn't want to tell even to her own self.

She hear a voice, raw and loud, calling out, 'Ello, ello, mawnin' from behind her as if the person trying to attract her attention in particular. She wipe her hand on a piece of cloth and limp slow and painful to the door, almost revelling in this last opportunity afforded by the advent of a caller to let her movements succumb to the pain a moment before she had to slip on the mask again.

She push her head through the wash area doorway and look to the right and then to the left. She don't see anybody at first for her eye dark and the sunglare in her face, but she say, 'Yes?' and same time a woman shape detach from the shadow in the corner and the voice come again, 'Mawnin mam. Hah looking for apartment number 10B. You can tell me is where?' Miss Minnie step out into the clear.

The minute Miss Minnie see the face she know something wrong, for her head grow and cold bump come up on her spine like when somebody trail ice down inside your frock neck and it take a while to touch you but you can feel it steadyin and touchin every space of air between the cloth and the skin before it lan.

'Who you come to?' Her voice come out unintentionally aggressive, but she don't like the feeling she getting down her spine, and is not prejudice, though still when say so she don't like them dancehall-looking type. The woman solid and big bone, not tall but taller than Miss Minnie, look like early or late forties, and she wearing a pink mesh blouse over a cream merino, and a rust-grey hobble skirt that just reach her knee. She have her head in a red braid wig what she tie back with a piece of pink ribbon like she never have time fi braid the braid so she just tie it back. The skin fair and thick and the face kinda look live in, hard and tired. But she wearing a bright red lipstick and she look like she woulda answer you back if you say anything she think slightly fresh. She wearin the dancehallish clothes but she look neat and well put together, and her whole body look brisk like she don't use to wasting time. She screw up her face like she not too please how Miss Minnie ax the question, but more like she confuse, is what dis? What wrong wid the ole lady, ehn?

'You know de hapartment, mam?'

'Yes, Ah know the apartment, but I want to know who you want there.'

'But see here sah. Why, you live there?'

'Yes, Ah live there. That's why I ask you.'

'Ah-oh. So is not there Mr Raymond Peddie live?'

Miss Minnie get more uneasy for she don't too like the sound of this woman, she never see Ray talk to that type any at all, but she say to herself that if is trouble she come fi mek, if Ray get himself involve in any parangles with some low-class woman, she really don't know how this going to go for if the woman get aggressive she don't even have her knuckleduster with her, she leave it upstairs under the mattress. Still, she want to get militant, like when you not sure if is duppy or is ole naygar but you not taking any chance, you making you challenge heard in case this whoever person think you is soft and come to advantage you.

At the same time she don't want to rude off to none of Ray friend for that can bring problem that hard to sort out. So she say, 'Yes, is there him live but him not there now, him gone to work from mawnin. You wants to leave a message, you can leave it.'

The woman was surveying her with a hard intent stare.

'Yes. Hi want to leave a message, I have it right here for im might really gone to work and I don't find 'im.' She hold out a small white envelope that kinda crease up a little bit. Miss Minnie take the envelope, making a great show of studying the writing for she letting this loud-looking stranger know she can read, even though in truth and in fact she can't.

The woman still watching her. 'So what is your name? You is him helper or him relative?'

'I is not no helper. I is him modda.'

The woman don't answer. A silence, a kinda weighted-ness, descend like something throw down on the ground between the two of them. The woman studying Miss Minnie with her hard bright stare as if she contemplating between options. Miss Minnie returning the stare.

Finally, the woman say, 'Awright'. And again, 'Awright', as if she make up her mind sudden bout something. 'Beg you give him the letter soon as him come fi me, for it very important. Is somebody hax me to deliver it fi dem.'

Miss Minnie come out in the yard and watch the woman back till she disappear under the guard rail that the guardie lift up for her to pass through into the road. When she go upstairs she put the letter careful careful on Ray dresser and go back to her work, but the whole day the white envelope sitting there in front her eye like a accusation, and she almost tempted fi open it except she was never the type to get inside people privacy, and she don't grow Ray that way.

When Ray come in the evening she dish up him dinner as usual, and when him finish eat and cock up him foot on the settee to watch the news, she say to him, casual casual like she just announcing that dinner ready, 'Letter on the bureau for you.'

'Thanks, Mamma.' He get up same time and go into

65

the room and she strain her ears and she hear when the envelope rip, and then she don't hear anything for a long time. Miss Minnie sit down back on the settee for she feel weak all of a sudden.

After a long time Ray come out the room and say, 'Mamma, Ah goin out. Ah soon come back.' She look at him face but it blank blank, clean and smooth as a sheet. She open her mouth to say, 'Son, yu awright?' but then she say to herself she jus frighten fi bush, taking shadow fi duppy, so she keep quiet and watch him pick up him car key and walk through the door.

When him reach the door him fling back casual casual over him shoulder, him not showing him face, 'Miss Minnie, is who bring the letter?'

'One stout brown woman inna skirt and blouse. Say somebody give her to give you.'

Him never say anything to her for three week. She never bother tell him she leaving yet for she have this strange feeling like she waiting, waiting for something that her spine kinda sense but her brain don't make no connection underneath it yet. Then one evening when him come in him don't eat him dinner. When she ax him if she must share it out, him say no. Him sit down on the settee with the TV remote in him hand and she watching him but him switching from station to station and when him steady on one station for a few minutes him eye not really on the picture, it flitting all over the place like him travelling. She sitting in the corner shelling the peas for next day dinner on a piece of newspaper she put on the carpet but she not saying nothing, she just watchin him. Then all of a sudden him get up, sudden so like somebody jerk a string under him ribs bone, and him walk over to where she sitting and stand up over her.

'Mamma, Ah want talk to you.'

Miss Minnie keep her voice serene. 'What you want talk to me bout?'

Him sit down beside her and for a good while him don't answer. Then at last him put him hand in him trousers pocket and take out a photograph, a small two by four, and hand it to her without speaking.

Miss Minnie study the picture for a long time. She don't say anything. After a while she lay it careful on the chair on her other side and go on shelling peas.

'Mamma, you remember the woman who come here the other day with the letter?'

'Yes, Ah remember.' Miss Minnie voice still serene. 'Is me modda.'

'You eyebone and you walk is the dead stamp of her,' Miss Minnie say.

◆

The note simply said, 'If you want to meet your mother, call this number.' Inside it was the photograph. The note was unsigned.

At first he thought he wouldn't do anything. But for days the note and the photograph just keep shifting in and out his mind like water lapping between stones, hiding and then showing itself. Some days he just sit there looking into space till at work they start asking him if he's well. He wondering if is a trick or what. He tell himself it don't really matter but deep in him belly him feel the chicken them that coming home to roost. Him belly feel funny and when him try to eat sometimes the food can't go down.

So she alive then. If is really she. So why she keep quiet

67

all these years, what she up to why she suddenly surfacing now? He hoped she didn't think now he was working he had anything to give her for all he have is for Miss Minnie.

All his life Miss Minnie had been sufficient. But sometimes sitting in the shadows in his father's shop, he wished his father would cuff him over the head the way Maas Baada and the other men did. And at night in his dreams there was this girl with long slim dancer's legs who beckoned to him and laughed and laughed and laughed, laughing at him but in a nice way so he wasn't embarrassed at all. 'What you fraid for? You fraid o' me? Cho man, don't fraid. Ah not going to do you anything.' And she laugh and laugh and laugh and laugh, a whole pealing carnival of laugh creasing up her face and she throwing back her face in the sun to laugh because he too paralyse with shyness and love to come to her. When she beckon him she fling out her arms like a dance, and they long and slim like her legs, dancing in the air like scarves.

All his girlfriends had long slim dancer's legs and arms and throats that glowed when they threw their heads back to laugh. The people in the district use to say, 'Boy, you is the dead stamp of you mother. Can't understand how she up and lef you like that … But you know, don't worry youself. Boy pickni favour they mother always lucky like bitch. You going be one lucky fella.'

One day in school the teacher say, 'Today is Mother's Day. I am going to show you how to draw a Mother's Day Valentine to your mother.'

Vassell Burgess take his suck finger out his mouth and give out, 'Miss, miss, Raymond Peddie don't have no mother to write Valentime to. Him mother run 'way lef him gone dance go-go, is Miss Minnie is him modda.' Then he put the suck finger back in him mouth and continue feeling him navel under him shirt.

In the yard at recess he fight Vassell Burgess for scandalling his mother. Man Teacher give him three lash.

But he didn't really think about her at all. It had never made any sense to him to think about her all these years, for it was clear she had never wanted him. She never want him. He stand between her and go-go, like fog and high rise between a crying child and stars.

His strongest urge was to dismiss the letter as a hoax. But it stay there niggling like a worm that boring into a mango and in the end he take out the letter and read it again trying to bore holes with his eyes into the handwriting. The writing big and round and semi-literate, like somebody write it who leave school in Grade Nine. It look real.

◆

She nervous like fahleetee but she dead if she go let anybody know. When they call her from round the front of the club say a young man come to see her, she know is who immediately. She wipe her hands on her apron, take off the apron slow and careful and easy easy, smooth her hair in the flyblow mirror on the kitchen wall, wipe a spot of lipstick like blood from off her front teeth, spread her mouth wide in a parody of a smile and wiggle it to get her face muscle relax, and go out in the front to meet him.

He was standing on the patio among the umbrellaed tables and chairs with his back to the club entrance, a tall thin young man in firecoal grey slacks and a soft cream polo shirt, his shoulders hunched and the neck drawn down between the shoulders as if to protect himself from an impending blow or the cynosure of eyes. His back was to her but she would have known him anywhere. The long lean spine was hers as a young girl, she get it from her own father, Long Man Talbot. The sleek graceful headback with the hair growing low down on the neck way below where other people's hairline stopped, was something that run in her family from way back. She herself had to shave her legs every week and pick hair out of her chin with tweezers every day.

He had chosen his time well. There was no one else on the patio. The club didn't open its doors to patrons until five. It was barely one o'clock.

She stood for a moment watching him pretending he didn't know she was there, then she made up her mind briskly, sharply, as was her custom.

'Ray.'

He spun round at that, balanced on the heel like a dancer, or someone disturbed.

'Raymond.' His voice was harsh, aggressive, uncertain. 'My name is Raymond.' Ray was Miss Minnie's name for him.

She shrugged, not dismissively. 'Awright. Raymond then. Come siddung nuh.'

She walked between the tables to one just at the pool's edge, not looking back to see if he was following. He watched her helplessly, shocked by a sudden, overwhelming access of rage so that wetness like blood filled his eye sockets and for a moment he could not see. But even then he registered her body's brisk, stolid swiftness in which he could find no trace of the slim dancer of his dreams. She was just a thickset woman whose body had been too lived in. Probably by too many others, he thought cynically as he made his way towards her among the tables, picking his way carefully and fastidiously so that their edges did not touch him or contaminate his hands. The whole time he was moving she never took her eyes off him, her stare bright and hard like enamel and a little smile playing at the corner of her bright red smudged mouth like a dancehall Mona Lisa, slightly ironic, slightly mocking, slightly challenging, lost. He wanted to wipe the smile off her face with a clean handkerchief.

He sat, feeling unmoored. In none of his past existence had feeling been more turbulent or more complex than water running under stone, smooth and quiet as buried bone. He didn't know what to do with this confused knot of emotion that he was on the surface of his head carefully tying up into a masculine ball and putting away in his pocket. Putting away in his pocket a thing that he knew was possessed. Possessed. A matrix of demons that with arcane lives of their own would roll out the pocket at any moment and knot his feet to these iron chair legs fastened to the ground under the white umbrella.

He looked at her directly, conscious of right on his side. 'So what I mus call you?'

She met him head on, stare for stare. The half smile continued to play around her lips even as they formed words.

'Is up to you. Whatever you want to call me. I not pushing anything.'

He didn't answer. They sat silent for a long time while he looked out over the blind blue of the pool's surface barely shifting in its stagnant circle. He locked his gaze so that he tuned her out of its frame. He watched the barely shifting water until he could make out another flow of its movement under the dappling sun. It was rocking itself, rocking itself, rocking itself like an old lady or a hammock, and he watched it till he felt it drawing him in. He watched an ant climb up

71

over his pants leg and bob and weave its way all the way up to his shirt front and try to burrow into his skin between two buttonholes. He reached out his hand and crushed it between forefinger and thumb, brushing his hand off on the firecoal pants.

'So what mek you turn up after all this time? What you want?' He didn't feel like making it easy for her.

She laughed through her nose, acknowledging the insult.

'As Ah tell you on the phone, Hi don't want anything except to see you.' She hesitated, then seemed to make up her mind about something. 'Ray, look, Ah know this not easy for you either, but this no really call for, you know. We is two big people, we really can't deal like pickni business.'

It was her way. Quick and direct and brutal as a knife. She didn't think the situation called for gloves, she wanted to foster no illusions in him about herself.

She offended him. With her lack of penitence, her absence of sobriety.

'It is a pickni business,' he said, rough and scornful. Then, as if ashamed of exposing himself, quiet, emotionless, 'That's why we here, isn't it?'

'Yes. Fi real.' She looked at him sideways, her voice gone soft, gentle, shocking him. 'What you need, Ray? You need me to explain why I lef you?'

'Need? Is you send call me you know lady.'

She laughed again in her nose and her throat, saying Touché. 'Yes, that is true. Is me send call you. When it said and done is really me need you.'

That shock held him frozen, still. If she wasn't the kind of woman who could speak soft and gentle (her raucous lived-in body and raw tones had no corners or curves for whispers) even less was she the kind of woman who admitted need. Such things belonged to finer feelings. She wore red braid the colour of hardwood floor dye, and thrust her breasts forward like a dancehall queen when she walked, so that even though she was covered she was exposed. She didn't seem to realize she was a big woman and not a young girl.

If he didn't move now it was because he couldn't, not because he tuned her out to process static. He was held still in a cylinder of waiting.

'Ray. Mek me tell you the truth.' She felt him wince without his giving a physical sign. 'Me know you don't want me to call you Ray because it must be soun too friendly or what, and you don't really know me. But is hard for me to get use to the Raymond part for is me name you, an' Ray is what Hi call you the twelve months I keep you. Is what Ah call you in me mind all the time, it not going go 'way so quick overnight.'

She didn't really expect him to respond. 'But mek Ah tell you the truth. Hah know exactly what the country people them tell you, for Ah know how them talk. An' me not telling you any lie, Ah really do what them say. Ha couldn't tek the tie-down business so Ah lef. Is the truth.'

The baldness fell on the tiles between them, waiting to be picked up. He sat processing the feel and tone and texture of the words that had already disappeared, feeling them through her voice's remnants as a blind man fingers sound, shaping it between finger and thumb for texture and nuance and grain and wear.

He told himself he hadn't really expected to hear anything else, except lies.

'So is me tie you down?' It was half statement, half question, half accusation. Three halves, out of sync.

She answered without hesitation, like someone who had either rehearsed or had decided not to hide.

'No, is not you tie me down. But Ah couldn't cope with you father. Ah jus never know how to live with a man who never talk. Ah jus couldn't deal with it.'

He could feel her struggling to read the spaces in his silence, decode him with her own fingertips of feeling, and he felt a surge of malice that she pissing herself with swallowing all this graveyard water that rising over the bridge.

'Ray, boy, you wouldn't understand. Hi don't even want to try to make you understand, for I not here making excuse for myself, but I jus couldn't live with the man. I pregnant fi nine month, feeling big and bloated and ugly, vomiting all over the place, and the man clean me and feed me and mind me, and if him change two word with me fi the nine month, is plenty. Him was a good man, but is not that I did want. I feel like I tie down in a cage like bird that people feed and keep like pet. I leave you with him because I know I couldn't take care of you where I was going. Hi didn't even know where I was going. But I know him woulda did take care a you, for him did love you. Only thing, Hi pray to God Almighty day and night begging Him that when Lester find a woman, for him is a man that can't live without woman, is one that woulda take care a mi pickni.'

Lester. The shock of his father's name on her lips jolted him. Lester. Yes, Lester. Is so him did really name. He hadn't thought of it, had seldom heard it, in years. His father's name was Lester. Everybody called him Shoey. Including Miss Minnie. Aside from that, he never seemed to have any name.

He used to wish his father would talk to him more, or even cuff him over the head with a curled palm the way Maas

Baada and others of the men did. When it never happened, he told himself Miss Minnie was sufficient.

His father had died as silently as he had lived, lying down in his bed one morning and sleeping off instead of rising early to go to the field before opening the shop as he used to do. The autopsy said he had suffered a heart attack. Everybody was surprised, for he was a thin strong man who had never had a day of illness that anyone could remember. Just as how nobody remembered him having a name.

Her voice began to change, sawing between loud and low as if she trying to chart and catch up with the ebbs and flows of meaning hidden in his not speaking.

'Ha didn't want to leave you. Tell you the truth Ray, it was the hardest thing I ever do in my whole life before or since. You was the one thing that make me life feel like smaddy polish it. But Ah couldn't cope with you father. Ah jus couldn't.' She said it again like a mantra, seeking to find the space of his understanding. 'But you turn out good, boy. Ah proud a you. Right now, Ha don't really have no agenda. Ha jus say to meself, Ah want a chance to make it up, if it possible. And if it not possible, if you coulda gimme a chance to be a part a you life in some way, Ah woulda glad same way. But if you don't want to see me no more, I wi understan the runnins. No sweat.'

She had become loud, and he felt revulsion and pity. He looked away from her young girl's bosom that had begun slightly to heave. But side on he notice that the hand she using to light up a Benson and Hedges sweat and kinda shaking.

At first Ray thought he would do nothing about her. Now he had met her, his curiosity was satisfied. The book could be closed. Without complications. She had, as she said, made no demands, and he had acceded to none.

He would do nothing about her. But that was not strictly true. He did a great deal in his mind. An irritating, nagging need to name her kept worrying away at the recesses of his mind. With grim humour, he thought of her as the other woman. Then as the Prodigal Returned. But prodigal meant lavish giver, and what had she given? Nor had she been penitent. Both on the phone during their first conversation and later at the club where she worked, she had stated bald facts, asking for and giving no pity. She had not said she had had a change of heart about abandoning him, indeed, he felt she would do the same again if the situation was now. Her attitude was that she had thought of herself and of him both, and had done what she thought was best for both. She did not say she had not contacted him all the years because she didn't want to confuse him or cause conflict. She didn't say any of the things he expected her to say to justify her effrontery in seeking him out at this stage. It was as if she was totally insensitive or unconscionably proud, leaving it up to him to bridge the yawning space of her pride with questions that he refused to ask. He felt that she had asked him to meet her more than halfway when it was her responsibility to walk towards him all the way. He would not do it.

Mostly in his mind he thought of her simply as 'her'. He could not bring himself to say the word 'mother'. The contradiction of this was not lost on him, since all his life he had thought of her as his mother. There was a certain perversity, he knew, in feeling that now he had met her, discovered that she lived in the flesh and was real, he was no longer able to invest the word with any proper meaning.

He felt that he had no real relation to her, yet he found himself relieved that she was a cook, not a dancer, at the club. Relieved that it was quite a decent, even reputable, club. She had given him her address in lower Kingston, and though he had no intention of visiting her there, he was relieved too that while it was not an address that would appear in the *Gleaner's* Who's Who, it was not in Riverton City. It set him free from any lurking responsibility to offer her financial support. If it occurred to him that the most obvious possibility was that he felt her to be a part of him and himself to be a part of her, he did not dwell on the thought.

He felt that her most profound impact had been on his relationship with himself, the way he thought about himself in the world, and his attitude to that world. He had no words or evidence to describe this feeling, except to say that he felt like a man who had discovered late one night that there was another person in the bed with him, not outside under the covers but inside under his skin, sharing it with him. A terrible whisper of habitation with a ghost or a Siamese twin with which he coped by shelving the thought of what the relationship might mean, but every night forced to get under the covers with this devilish presence sharing his skin, whispering things he was not ready to hear, nudging him in private parts with obscene hands that had no right yet every right to touch him there, since his private parts belonged to it also.

He didn't say anything to Miss Minnie, though it made him feel guilty to withhold this from her. Yet his guilt about the duppy twin he could not name also kept him silent. But

Miss Minnie was no fool. One evening after dinner when he went to watch TV she just collared him.

'So is when you plannin to tell me bout you lady modda?'

She took him so by surprise, he defended himself with a lie.

'Tell you what bout her? I don't business with her. I not having anything to do with her.'

'You havin everything to do with her.'

'No.'

'Oh yes? Is that why you talking in you sleep and steppin roun the house like somebody tie you up with elastic so you can hol up in one piece?'

He was speechless. Miss Minnie didn't bat an eye.

'Best way to deal with it is either accept it or get her outa you system.'

He spoke bitterly, sarcastic. 'And how do you propose I do that, ma'am?'

She refused to rise to the bait of his English. 'Why you don't invite her roun for dinner one evening?'

And so began Raymond Peddie's curious courtship of his mother. It took the form mainly of casual telephone calls he made to her, not too often, just to show her he was a big man and understood about water under bridges. She came to the house only once, to thank Miss Minnie for looking after her son. She brought a present, a beautiful set of crockery that surprised him with its expense and taste for he didn't know she knew the quality of things. 'Ha can't pay you for what you do for me son,' she said, 'han' I wouldn't even try. This is jus a likkle tenky. I wish it was more, but Ah hope you can find some use for it.'

She called him sometimes, not too often, just to ask

how he was doing and to see if Miss Minnie was well. But for some reason she would not come to the house. Eventually he visited her once at her house, and met the man she was living with and his two brothers, Sam and Nichol, who had been born after him from a different father, not her current man. It was strange to think he had brothers, that it was not him alone in the world. Stranger still to think they had always known of his existence, while he had never known of theirs. He discovered in himself an excitement and a thirst for this relationship, and they welcomed him both with curiosity and as if he had been a mere extension of themselves. Neither had received his education, but they could read and write and had both been as far as Grade Eleven in secondary school. Sam was a mechanic earning good money at his own garage, and Nichol ran a taxi on the Three Miles route. They were more glad than proud of his achievements, glad that he had made something of himself but comfortable with their own freedom and vaguely if affectionately contemptuous of an education that denied him his. Sam was living in his own half-finished two bedroom with his baby mother, Maxine, and Nichol was still living at home but saving to buy a piece of land.

It was through his brothers that he came to see his mother in a different light. To him she was the absence that had never left him, but also the knot in his stomach that refused to unravel and let him easily answer the question of what kind of man he was. His dislike was mixed with a reluctant admiration for the way she held her corners, her unspoken insistence that he take her on her own terms, as he found her now, not as he had imagined her in the past. By setting him the impossible task of beginning a relationship at the point where they had met, she kept him tied to her, for how could he walk away from understanding this enigma that defied the forms of motherhood?

His fascination repelled him as did her blatant sexuality that refused to acknowledge her age or her well-covered dancehall body. His brothers who had lived with her all their lives had no such struggles with her, only a teasing, easy affection that made her ordinary. He found that their influence helped him. He had started off wanting her, but their easy acceptance allowed her to become merely the occasion for his life with his brothers. It was they who made him feel ordinary, and sometimes almost whole.

◆

Years after when Raymond told me the story, he said the thing he could not understand was the way Miss Minnie change. Marlene, she jus start acting funny, he said. First she started waiting up for him no matter how late he come in. And these days he really coming in late, for he spending time with his brothers after work and he also now seeing a girl, and several nights a week he spending time late at her apartment or taking her out. But even up to one a.m. he would find Miss Minnie waiting up for him – she not saying anything but she sticking close in the small apartment and is as if she suspect him of something but she not asking and she not saying anything. He begin to feel stifle. He say, 'Miss Minnie, you don't have to stay up for me you know, I can take care a meself. You didn't use to do it before, so why you worry so now?'

'Kingston a bad place,' she say, 'an' Ah can't sleep knowing you out on the road them bad time a night.'

He know she want him to tell her where he was without

her asking, but he not telling her he was out having a drink and playing domino with his brothers.

He don't know if he imagining it but is like she shadowing him and sometimes he feel she behind the doors listening in on his telephone conversations. He shame to put a trap for her but sometimes he start opening the door sudden with the telephone still in his hand but he never catch her there, she always have her back to him dusting some piece of furniture that she dust all four time already for the day. He say to himself that maybe he really imagining it, maybe is just that all of a sudden she start looking like her old self again. She start back wearing the bright tie-heads that remind him of a bright lizard and he begin to wonder how he never notice it before, that she really move her body like a lizard.

He get a promotion and the company lend him money to pay down on a house and he tell Miss Minnie he go build her a house back in Baltree, he want her to go down and check out a spot and see how she can organize a place to stay so she can supervise the building. Miss Minnie say a thing he never like at all. She say, 'See it there, Jesus God be praise. No matter who try to come between me an' you, you is me old age pension. Everything you got is fi you one modda that raise you, God bless you, boy.'

He so frighten for Miss Minnie never talk like that before. In fact she always so proud and independent he never think she woulda look at him in that light, and when he put what she say together with how she stay long in the apartment and suddenly stop helping him with the food money from the little she have put by from the sale of the shoemaker business to Maas Baada grandson, him don't like it at all. But he too shock to say anything. He don't know what he coulda say.

Couple times well his mother give him things to give Miss Minnie, mostly food kind to help with the household expenses, but sometimes a fruit basket specially for herself, and on her birthday a lovely pair of soft shoes of the kind that constantly pleased and astonished him with her taste. Since the promotion and everything else he really busy, he hardly have time to notice anything, even the food he put in his mouth he just put in there and swallow like a automatic machine, so he don't really notice what, if anything, Miss Minnie doing with the things his mother send. But the morning after her birthday he taking out the garbage and he find the pair of leather shoes cut up fine fine and throw on top the rubbish as if she making sure he see it.

At first he couldn't really believe is the shoes but when he confront her and her face contort up like is somebody else behind the skin and she start froth and scream, he realize that something seriously wrong going on all this time behind the mask of her silence. She rant and rave say how she know him don't business with her, is the tough-ass go-go woman that leave him from he still shitting his nappy he spending all his time and money on now, after she Minnie done kill out her soulcase fi him, now the facety gal come sending her present like she think she is nobody and don't have anybody to look after her, but yes, is right she right, she mus right because no he give her reason to think that, but even though nobody don't business with her she is not no blasted pauper and she don't want no charity and nobody what lef.

'Tek it outa me house! Tek it outa me house!' she screamed, totally beside herself.

By the time he calm her down he so frighten he want to take her to doctor, but she refuse. She fall down weak on the ground and he help her up in her bed and she sleep off for almost a whole day, and when she wake up is as if nothing happen and she don't remember a single thing about what happen. He don't know if she pretending or she really forget but he really worried. She nice nice to him after that and cooking all his favourite food till nothing left in the house for the rest of the month. But still every little time he catch her watching him with that outa the corner of her eye slanty look that remind him so much of a watching lizard. He start doing his best to pay her more attention for he admit to himself with a guilty feeling that without realizing it he had been neglecting her, treating her like piece of the furniture while he spending more and more time with his girlfriend and his brothers. And he had not involved her in his relationships, partly because of the memory of when he used to bring people home – he felt he embarrassed her – and partly because for reasons he could not name he felt she would not have been comfortable with his brothers around so often. He start coming home earlier whenever he could, and he thinking he would be spending more time at home now for she don't like to go out, but he was wrong. Miss Minnie all of a sudden turn young girl and want him to take her everywhere, tour Kingston, dress up in her Sunday best. She seem happier and more contented but he still don't feel good because she still giving him the funny sideways glances and when he with her he just feel this feeling that she surrounding him, like she holding him to book for something that she waiting for him to give her. And sometimes she purse up her mouth like somebody deciding to fight for they right, the way she used to do when she don't know where the next cent coming from to send him to school and she determine he going anyway. If they were in the habit of talking close or touching each other he might have hugged her and they might have been able to sort out whatever it was that was eating her under the skin, but all he could do was just tease her out of her tightness with laughter and jokes. He couldn't say, 'Miss Minnie you don't have to be jealous you know, all I have is for you', because he felt that to say this would be to confess to a betrayal he had not committed, and moreover he felt that there was a level at which this was not true.

He don't tell his mother or his brothers any of this. The habit of silence was still strong in him, but more than this, in this situation he felt them as strangers. He felt that to speak of it would be a betrayal of Miss Minnie.

Soon after the incident the loan come through. She make the trip down to Baltree, he drive her down himself, and they make some contacts and he set up a thing so she can stay with Miss Florrie Green while the place building. He drive back to town feeling a shamed sense of relief for the little space and respite from this new Miss Minnie he don't know, not expecting to see her again for a little while, till the next time he go down to check on her and how the building going. Hnn. About two weeks later he come home to find Miss Minnie had let herself in with her spare key. The workmen run out of material so she say to herself let Ah come and help Ray with some of the washing and cleaning, poor thing, he don't have anybody to look after him for me is the one mother he got. And she looking at him sly and secret out the corner of she eye like green lizard.

Late that night he hear her crying to herself saying over and over, 'Is so. Is so. Is jus so. I don't have any use any more. Is so. Is so. Is jus so.' Ray so frighten he run outa the room into hers and hug her up tight tight tight for the first time since he was a little child and he himself start crying like a child. But she wouldn't listen to him when he really break and beg her not to think he go leave her or replace her with anyone. She jus hanging on to him and mourning over and over again, 'Is so. Is jus so. I don't have any use any more.'

Is that night Ray decide something really wrong, and he have to insist she go to the doctor.

The doctor say Miss Minnie suffering from extreme depression because she coop up in the town place that she not use to too long, plus the arthritis that she hiding from him that it getting worse making it hard for her to manage and it left her feeling low in her self-esteem. He say Miss Minnie is like a damage tree that hold up over plenty year, but it struck in the root and one day it jus can't stand the strain and everything jus give way. Ray know the doctor don't know the half of it but he don't tell him anything, he leaving him to find out for himself anything else Miss Minnie plan to let him know or guess.

At the time he telling me all of this Miss Minnie had finish getting doctor's care and well recover for over a year, and she living in the new house Ray build for her on a piece of lease-purchase land over across from Miss Florrie. He coming down to see her almost every weekend except month end when she go up or whenever he don't have to be on call at the workplace where he steadily moving up now, headed everyone said for the top job.

Miss Minnie quiet and keep to herself same as usual before she go town and develop her sickness, but is a mystery how rumour fly and naygar mouth set on corner, slightest little thing they fly off and they know everything in everybody life story and what they don't know they invent. Black Shop and Maaga Bay and Green Town people have it to say how Miss Minnie did mad in town because she visit Butty Cassells' obeahyard and put guzzum on Ray mother and it boomerang on her, the day she come down here saying she coming to visit old neighbour. Hnn. Which neighbour? After Minnie don't talk to nobody from I know her, she keep herself to herself from the day she land in Baltree till this day of our Lord.

Miss Minnie in the new pretty house and plenty people vex that she doing so well and plenty people glad that she finally reaping something from all the hard work she lavish on the boy that never come out her own belly, but Miss Minnie going on with her farming and her selling same way for she don't want to be a burden on Ray plus she like to keep active and the little extra money come in handy to stretch out the monthly upkeep that Ray insist she take from him. She going to her church and she busy and helpful there same how she used to be in the PTA when Ray was at school, and once a month she go up to town with a parcel of everything under the sun that she plant and bake to help out Ray so he don't have to buy every little thing, town things so expensive, and she helping him with the cleaning and the washing same way, taking her piece of cloth and her beeswax for town polish is foolishness, and still not using any washing machine because machine don't know when the clothes want blue.

Telling me this story was the only time Ray really bared himself to anyone. When he left I knew finally he never forgave me for hearing it, and when I did my own leaving it was because of a picture in my mind of us two standing on separate river banks, but beside him on one side was his father and on the other was Miss Minnie holding his hand. She met and liked me, but I knew Ray would never married to anyone as long as Miss Minnie alive, for he fraid any woman come between him and her again. Sometimes is like

86

her illness draw them together in a different way, like it open out a space where them is two equal human being trying to look after each other, not this larger-than-life woman and the little boy trying to live up under her skirt tail. I see them together and they tender to each other like two egg shell.

Yet still and all I don't know if is love or an indecent obsession holding him down so he can't stop making it up to her. I say to myself obligation is a hard master, for is a sea that never empty no matter how deep you drink and it leave him so dry he have no pillow to lie down with anybody to share his dreams. But he happy and Miss Minnie happy and I not taking on this emptiness, this space that hollow waiting for where a man ought to be. I know some of oonu will have it to say I not a reliable witness for I jealous Miss Minnie, but who feels it knows it, every tub siddung on its own bottom.

His leaving made me feel free to write it all down. Another act of betrayal, he might have said.

Still I have to admit some people really bad mind, like the ones that when they see Miss Minnie say, 'Hnn', like they feel they don't hear the end of the story.

MORRIS HOLE

You could reach the river if you went round by the long road through the woodland behind our house and the Wesleyan church. But that was the long road. Mostly we just use to skate down Jimbo Gully on coconut bunkers till we reach the crossing where the two tracks meet. After that you walk about a mile and a half through a big mango walk, where when mango time you had to step careful because of the whole lot of ripe mango just falling and rottening and sippling up the ground so if you not careful you slide and break something serious.

Till this day I don't know whether I love or hate the smell of ripe mango. Going through that mango walk in August and July, you got totally drunk with the smell, you either want to sleep or stop and eat mango like dirt. Usually you stop and eat mango like dirt. Sometimes there were bees, too, hordes of them, and then you better walk double careful unless you want to go back to school with a fat eye. People use to thief the honey, boil it down to wax and use it to shine they floor till it make looking glass shame. So most of the time the bees well vex, and they don't pardon nobody who walk careless that way.

Behind the mango walk was open pasture where Maas Baada cow and Mr Marcus horse colony use to feed. All the time you walking, you looking out careful in case you foot step on a leaf that shout out cris! crups! and Maas Baada big black bull cow hear and decide to chase you. Cow use to chase only female or if you wear red, so my brothers use to shout out, 'Sic 'im, bull cow, sic 'im!' every time we come near to the cow pasture, and no matter how my mother upset and threaten to switch them backside, it never make a difference.

As soon as we reach the bend in the road and see the first cow, 'sic 'im, bull cow, sic 'im!' and is gone them gone like lightning, it never make any sense my mother trying to catch them and bust they arse because she couldn't run with the washpan on her head.

The track open out sudden so in a sea of grass like rivermumma hair that just comb, and more cows, which you slide past fast but careful careful, really double careful, then you climb under a barb-wire fence and you reach the river, but you know you reach it long before you see it, just by the sound and the smell.

Smelling like how all river smell. That time when I was nine it was just river, I didn't know any other name but river for its smell. Now, distanced by memory and the rivers of older experience, I think of loam and birth and things growing at the root.

Smelling like river. Sounding like how all rivers sound. Like people talking, where the water buck and run over stone, the voice going up and down up and down like when my mother, Miss Clemmy, Miss Nellie, my cousin Munchie and her mother Miss Retinella Martin – the whole lot of Seventh Day Adventist lady – bending down on Sunday morning beating the clothes on the rockstones and calling conversation to each other across the surfaces of pools. But when it run smooth and quick where it don't have no stones, it more like the earth talking with itself, or singing to a baby that don't yet born. Dark and deep and murmuring, like a murmuring tucked away in the belly inside. Soft and low like the baby not yet born.

◆

Morris Hole River. Here we grew up, very fast. Very very fast. But before that, we were children, growing down.

◆

This is where the first time my mother tell me, 'Go put on you clothes and stop the running up and down with boy pickni, if I ever catch you do that again I switch you behind for you.' It was the last day of my nakedness and my first memory of grief.

◆

Collages. Night in our house under the banking and the nine of us keeping up carousing so bad, jumping up and down in the bed just to hear it going cricru-shshsh! Cricru-shshsh! Cricrushshsh! like some muffled underground dancehall, keeping up carousing so bad my father coming in five times for the night with the strap, so we had to dive head first either into the bed or under it, revelling in its cricru-sh cricru-sh cricru-sh! sound even as we dodging from the licks my father threatening but not giving.

Images slide under, beneath and across each other, an impressionist's pallet of nakedness half remembered, lost. The open space of grass before the woodland, we called it Pan Land, Pan Land and here is we climbing up to the tip top of the long thin grape tree when the wind blowing wild, singing and rocking to the rhythm of how the tree shiver. In the wild wind flying paper-and-coconut-bone kites with ole cloth for streamers. Grabbing coconut bunkers and skating down to Jimbo Gully at the speed of greased lightning, till we couldn't pretend any more that our mother's shouting at us to come there had blown away on the wind. So we haul up our coconut bunkers like weary, satisfied fishermen towing their boats to shore with care, pushing them up under our armpits to take away for safekeeping. Trailing home reasonable happy even though we know is watercarrying from 'Ccasion Call and bathing for the night waiting for us, pure horrors because 'Ccasion Call far and the kerosene tins heavy, and because after you roll in grass you don't want no water touching your skin, for hell scratch out your daylights all night wholenight.

The lost eye slides between one shadowed dream of outlines and another, loses itself either in the heart's truth or memory's constructed romance. Sliding across its skin is the truth or the memory of the road from school after the rain fall and every puddle under the sky become pickni paradise. But you still pick and choose, so you push your puss boot into the muddiest puddle you can find and listen for the sweet sweet satisfying sound of 'squish, squiddish, squish, glupps', and if you wearing real shoes you take them off and make your bare toes do the work instead, and even though you know bust arse coming tonight when your mother ask you how your shoes wet and your clothes soak, you don't too mind for paradise worth every sacrifice of skin.

Images give way to sound, single bright filaments, swelling into thread, then single bright roots and scatters and swells and syncopates of song. The school yard at recess time, Brownie time, Scout time and Girl Guides time. The whole yard shining and loud where we played rabbit in the hollow run, singing there was a man name Nathan Stone, he had a goat that he called his own, singing I went to the animals fair, the birds and the bees were there, the monkey fell off his monk, and fell on the elephant's trunk, singing waltzing matilda, waltzing matilda, watching fight bust, shoot marble, swap taw, fight boy, quarrel over whose turn with the skipping rope.

◆

So I sing you a song of losing the river.

All this I lose when my mother say what she say and I lose the river.

◆

I feel so shame, I feel as if the earth could open and take me in. Why my Mother say that, man, when she never say such a thing before? Every Sunday I rip off my clothes as soon as we sight the river and all of we screaming down the river course grabbing crayfish under rotten leaf in the water under the almonds tree, racing from river stone to river stone till we reach Blue Hole and dive in to show off or throw split bamboo in the water to catch mullet and eel. Eating rose apple that our mother say we mustn't eat because it poison at certain season, but we can't leave it alone for it grow too lush on the river bank to let die without hungry belly visit it. Why she say that, and is as if the sun drop out of the sky and everywhere dark for not to play in the river is like you might as well dead or be bigpeople then, but I shame shame because the way she say it I know is because something wrong with me. My heart full like it going burst, like I swallow one big everlasting mug of water and it stop between my throat and my chest and I can't breathe good, and I put on my clothes under a dumb cane bush that scratch me till I nearly mad afterwards.

I feel I will never be able to play again, my whole body amputate.

♦

One day my cousin Munchie and her mother Miss Retinella come to the house and Miss Retinella say to my mother, 'But how this likkle one mekking bubby aready? You sure she not seeing boy?' My mother screw up her face the way she usually screw it up when somebody talking something she don't like but she too polite to tell them so direct, but the way her face make up and her voice squeeze up like suck orange, is only somebody like Miss Retinella who have a skin like a rhinoceros coulda miss how she vex.

'No sah,' she answer Miss Retinella short short and her voice sounding funny like suck orange and like she go cry all in one, 'no such thing.'

When Miss Retinella continue on the subject, 'But Ionie you have to careful with her you know, she showing woman now and boy will troble her', my mother just pick up her self-heater iron and walk off into the house to iron her clothes, leaving Miss Retinella and Munchie standing outside. That evening she was extra nice to me and the whole time she was hugging me up as if she crying, but she never say a word.

That is when I understand what wrong with me why my mother say don't play in the river. The girls in Six Class say I have kernel in them – all I know was they swell up and hurt and keep knocking on everything I pass – chair pin, table edge, door jamb, every god almighty thing, my chest keeping up serious war with it all of a sudden, and is that Miss Retinella see and tell my mother I bad.

◆

Sometimes, early morning, we use to go down the river to bathe for school, so we could save the drinking water we fetch from 'Ccasion Call or Maniyenni the night before. If you go too early you had to wait for the sun to come up over the world's rim and send off the river mist before you go in the water, otherwise you could get arthritis pain and maybe even consumption. I use to like the early and the waiting for the sunrising because I thought the white fog, softer and tenderer than a dacron sheet, was the most beautiful thing in the world, and it didn't matter that it make the river icy cold. Somehow it seemed to fit. At the same time it scared your daylights, because when it coming up everything so still and quiet, was as if the fog like a blanket wrapping itself soft and merciless around the throat of sound, strangling it without even a whisper or a sigh. Nothing on earth could prevent you thinking a duppy was at your back, you could feel your head grow and the duppy hand trailing fingers like salted snail down your spine. Sometimes you feel the same way you feel when Effie spin, as if a whole set o' invisible people coming out from behind the trees on the river bank and standing there watching you, but you have a feeling that the ones on the river bank don't too like you, and you feel like how you feel when you passing underneath a silk cotton tree at dead of night.

Maybe they never mean to trouble me, but tell you the truth, I fraid from the word go because I don't like to wrap up with no duppy, so I glad my mother never let me go alone. But still I love the river.

My mother say the whole area surrounding the river use to be a district, but after many years and time change the young people move out to Green Town and Black Shop. Some of them go to Gutter Head and Maggotty and as far away as Mount Peace. My great-grandmother on my mother side, Sister Sis who didn't know who my grandfather's father was and give him to Maas Gussie Burgess when all the time his real name should have been Kitson, use to live there. 'Ta Sis', my mother use to hiss her teeth and say in her dark underneath voice that she use when she scorn what you do, 'Ta Sis, dark as middle night, no sense at all. She don't even know who is M'Pa father. You look pon Gussie Burgess and look pon we, you see any way a brown man like Gussie can have pickni black like M'Pa?'

'So who is Grampa Eric real father, Mamma?' we would ask again and again, each time she say it, as if the story new and we have to hear it again all over for the first time.

'Kitson, we is Kitson,' my mother say.

We didn't know who Kitson was because my mother say, 'You wouldn't know them. Is some people use to pass through the district,' and we had to satisfy with that.

But is Maas Gussie, who we knew, that interested us.

'So Maas Gussie own Grampa?' we would ask, as if we didn't know.

'Chups!' my mother sucked her teeth. 'Own what? You see Gussie paying oonu any mind when oonu pass him on the road?'

We lived again the exciting shiver of our disappointment, every time she said those words.

Maas Gussie was a very pretty man, tall and brown with nice hair, who lived in Maaga Bay near Miss Lilla big shop. Miss Lilla was the biggest shopkeeper in our district and she too was brown. We always greet Maas Gussie whenever we see him, as it was expected to do – not to greet a bigperson on the road was unheard of, the height of bad manners, for which you would earn a severe bust arse if it was ever reported. Maas Gussie was a very kind and affectionate man and he always answer us, just as he would answer any of the other children on the road. But he never say anything special to us.

People in our district use to talk free about children in families who were jacket or bad begetten, and nobody made these things a big deal unless they and you fall out and they going to cuss you. But always there was the unspoken knowledge that it was a disgrace, waiting coil up at your foot like a snake sleeping ready to strike if anybody should decide to cuss you. We never saw ourselves as jacket or bastard. Maybe it was because nobody except my mother that I remember ever talk about our wrong getten great-grandfather, and she only talk about it to us. My mother didn't cultivate friend, she keep to herself all the time, so you can see why is only we she tell. Maybe is because only we know, or maybe is because we hear Maas Gussie was our greatgrandfather before we hear he was only a jacket one, and the first impression stick, why we never shame. I only speculating, I still don't really know. All I know is that we never shame.

Sister Sis die long before we born so everything we know about her we know from what my mother say. I use to imagine her bending down in the riverside, one dark, bend-down black woman wrap up in black with black sheet over her head, washing the little black baby in the river and sometimes at night in my dreams when I cry out and my mother wake me, I get up and say, 'Eel run over him.' My mother never describe Sister Sis but I form my own impression. And I use to wonder how she never know whose the baby was, if duppy use to trouble her, for I didn't really know how babies came, except that they came through your navel, the disgraceful ones through their mother's bottom, but some of us, the lucky ones, came up through the mouth.

Wasn't just my great-grandmother on my mother's side who had all sort of strange thing about her, my mother use to give out dark utterance about my father's mother too, when she and my father quarrel. My mother say she was mad and I wondered if that mean mad like strange or like the woman with no name or mad like Netta Purcell who get off her head and go to asylum and come back but never quite regain her full faculties. But I knew better than to ask, as if I bareface about listening to bigpeople argument. Long after when I learn to cull up and stitch together the threads between what observe and what leave unsaid, I put two and two together make five, and come to realize my father's mother mad because she almost white but she only like black men.

She never know who she suppose to like.

I work this out because my father, my two uncles Easton and Alfred and my Aunt Beatrice, who had mostly different fathers, was full black, but my great-grandfather white as sea salt and my great-grandmother have two long jackass rope of hair wrap round her sambo head like black tobacco.

◆

I was too young to know the meaning of hate, so I just use to cry when my father say on our way from school we must stop by Mummah and Puppah and say howdy, for we have to have manners and respect for the older head. This was when we use to go to school in the next district, Maggotty, where Mummah and Puppah live on thirty acres of land, because Mamma never sure she should send us to the school in our real district because we had just moved to there and she was still sizing up things.

All I could hold inside my head was the shame and the fraid when me and Magsie walk up on their verandah, knock on the front door and wait long long like we begging, before Puppah come out the house, a short, white, cantankerous man with a voice like a dog bark and a little squinty blue eye that run water. It seem he just couldn't stand still, his whole body use to vibrate like he planning to have fits. He use to jerk himself from one foot to the other, which increase our feeling that he really never want us there. His voice scared me, but the part that shame us bad bad was how he never remember who we were.

'Evenin, Puppah.' We always saying this standing on tiptoe to run as soon as the words out of our mouth.

'Is who oonu?' he would bark, squinting and impatient, and while I stand there feeling the ground must be forget how to open from Bible days done, Magsie say, 'Is Papa send we to say howdy, Puppah. Maas Barber.'

'Oh, Barber pickni. Barber pickni. Awright, oonu gwan now.' And he would start off back inside his house. Sometimes, depending on the feeling, Magsie say, 'Papa say we mus say howdy to Mummah too.' Sometimes we never had the courage to complete the ritual, but mostly we did for when we go home, Papa asking you, 'You say howdy to Puppah?'

'Yes, Papa.'

'You say howdy to Mummah?' and you dared not say 'yes' when is no, for if he ask Puppah and hear is lie we telling, goose cook and backside roast with tamarind switch that night.

Going in to say howdy to Mummah was worse than

five of Puppah roll into one, for she was sick and always in her bed, a huge half tester with canopy and frill curtain like Queen inna barge on Egyptian Nile, and the room pack up with pure medicine bottle and pill bottle all over the place on wall bracket and shelf and bureau, and that is how I come to know how sickness smell. Mummah sit up in the bed looking like a witch in one thick pad up pad up pink duster and her hair in the black jackass rope round her head, and if you think is Puppah vex when we come, you never see Mummah, her face make up like Rainstorm and if she answer us when we say, 'Evenin, Mummah' is long time ago and I can't remember.

After every time we complain bitterly to our mother, and she in turn quarrel bitter bitter with my father, but it was the one thing she couldn't get her way with with him. Mostly he use to take whatever she say, but on this one thing he was adamant in a way I could never understand, because I knew our father loved us. Later I suspected my father was hoping they would remember to give us some kind of inheritance the way they never give him. Now I don't think that any more, I think he was hoping that when they saw us they would forgive him for running away, for when all is said and done the old man was the only father he knew. But when I was nine and had to go look in the old man's face every day coming from school, all I could hold inside my head was the shame and the fraid when me and Magsie walk up on their verandah knock on the front door and wait long long like we begging.

Strangely enough, these encounters never coloured my view of their daughter, my father's mother. The things my mother said remained buried in the bottom of my head, same like how the river bury and caress its secrets and roll stone over them. What I remembered was how my father talk about her. She died before we born but he talk about her so much that she became real, realer than my mother's frown and her dark prophecies about my grandmother's madness and consumption.

'Her skin clear, and she use to have two big long pretty plait of hair wrap round her head, same like Mummah,' he use to tell us, 'and she bury in a long white frock. Up to now I still see her in that long white frock.'

Afterwards I see my grandmother duppy with the two long pretty plait and the white eyelet frock like is her wedding.

My father said, 'I never know me father but I know him come from Port Maria.'

My grandmother die early and my father grow my two uncle, Easton and Alfred, and send them to school. He himself never really get any schooling because all the black grandoffspring had to work day and night on Puppah plantation. My father run away when he get a trade as a mason and take his brothers with him, because he didn't want them to see their name on bulla cake and eat it because they can't spell it, like how it happen to him.

◆

My head don't work straight like other people head. Sometimes my head weave stories inside itself, spinning a whole Anancy web of things that don't really go so but always feel realer than the things that go so. My Aunt Edna say is because my eye cast like hers, although you only notice the cast in my eye when I look at you sideways if you standing at a certain angle, whereas you can see hers clear clear. She say cast eye is a kinda mix up four eye, your brain don't come too straight.

100

I telling you all this to tell you how come my two grandmothers mix up in my head like that with the river and the day Munchie and Miss Retinella come and Miss Retinella tell my mother I bad. I didn't really start off planning to tell you about Sister Sis or my father mother but the two of them just creep inside my head and crawl out through my mouth like how some good begetten baby born. So I don't really push them out for they must be know what they doing in there. After all I swear Sister Sis still live in the riverbank and my other grandmother almost the same way like Sister Sis for although she seem to have no problem knowing who her children father was, she never know who she suppose to have them with and keep mudding up the white river between the lower parts of the districts and the upper.

I dream up in my head that sometimes I see them meet under the river bank washing the little black boy baby with the wrong father name together, and I dream up in my head that is their voice I hear when I sleep and hear the river washing over stone and calling conversation to itself across the singing pools. For they say duppy travel far and some duppy love river course, and between Morris Hole River and Maggotty where my father mother come from, is just a short journey if you follow the river course.

Sometimes when too much of the voices get mix up in my head I wonder if I suppose to act responsible and go see a shrink. But I know what they would say. They would say I have all sorts of trauma about my mother making me cruelly aware of my puberty. Among the voices that mix up in my head I can hear this prim, purse-up mouth voice sounding in my head, saying that it is all interconnected with the whispered, unsanctioned sexuality of my grandmothers, and me and my siblings' socially disapproved spawning from miscegenation.

That it all has to do with female shame and shaming. That the river becomes the connecting link because both Sister Sis and me lived there, because I was shamed into sexuality there, and because the river is female, a fountainhead of loamy juices like sex and birth where the rivermumma use to comb her hair and walk out on delicate feet into the cow pasture to spread the grass lips with her same silver comb. That legend and experience, social ritual and unconscious underground current of memory still living in my head and calling up my ancestors.

I really don't know about any of that. It sound too much like a English literature sociology class. All I know is I start out telling you the story about how I lose the river, and the rest of it get in the story and tell itself.

Anything you want think, you think, but in truth and in fact that is how we tell story where I come from, it don't haffi come straight for else it not sweet, and is just so it go.

When Cudjoe Man came to live in Baltree district, it was a nine days' wonder.

In those days people used to travel long distances in search of work, and anywhere night fell on you, that is where you rested – somebody in whatever place you found yourself would always give you a food and a bed for the night, and sometimes for many nights, if you found a work right there or on a property nearby and needed somewhere to stay. Sometimes people stayed and became part of the family, and that too was how people like my great-grandmother gave birth to children whose fathers' names became confused, and how stories about women like the one with no name, who had a child, Paul, by an unknown father, spread and flourished, fattening like love bush thrown carelessly across the tops of trees.

In those days whole districts used to lift up and change location, leaving behind empty spaces of green earth marked by sunken brown squares where houses used to be, green and brown and quiet except for the cooing of barble doves hidden behind the impenetrable face of trees. Empty spaces quiet with the hung weightedness – the breathless refusal to breathe – that always hovers over houses and places that have been recently deserted. The whole place standing still, refusing to grieve or give over to silence, in case the native changes his mind and returns.

It was a time of travellers. That vast and silent migration of people, not from country to town but from district to district and parish to parish, went unremarked because it was so much the stuff of our everyday lives, as instant and familiar as the minute-by-minute experience of touch and

103

conversation and the silent companionship of your own heart beating. Yet the movement was remarkable, as steady and significant as the flow of rivers or the swell of the sea. You met people on the road all hours of the day.

'Good morning, main, good morning sar, I hear they have work giving out on a property near by here. You know if is true?'

'Maybe yes, maybe no. So where you hail from?'

'I come from up the line, Trelawny. You ever hear of a place name Martha Brae?'

'Martha Brae? Martha Brae? Yes, I hear of Martha Brae. And who is your people?'

'Brissett. The name Brissett – Theophilus Brissett. Matter of fact my people come from down here long time now. Great-grandfather by my mother side by the name of Haughton – you know a man name Coziah Haughton?'

'But Lord a massy, you is Coz Haughton grandson? But see here, Coz daughter Heffie use to live just up the road there, just a stone throw from where I living. But is long time now she move out the district, gone to live at Point, her children take her over, for the poor thing get old now, can't manage herself so good again, especially since the hearing gone and doctor take off the foot, say she have sugar – you know, the diabetes – what they call the diabetes. But plenty of the man dem here work on Point property, so they can show you is where, her house not far from the roadside, easy easy to find. So you come to spend some time with your people then?'

Or you met them knocking on the corners of houses, all hours of night in the dark.

'Hol dog! Hol dog!'

'But see here, is who this at my gate this time of night?

What you want?'

'Just beggin a little drink of water, mam, comin from far.'

'Who is you? Tony, bring the bottle lamp so I can see this person that beggin water at the gate. Come out in the light mek me see your face.'

The light from the bottle lamp weaves and bobs, held high above the raised shoulder and the frowning brow, casting shadow over the waiting face.

'Well, you seem like decent person. But where you coming from this time of night, young girl like you? You not suppose to be walking road this late. Who is you? Who is your people? I don't know you from round here?' The last is a statement, framed as a question.

'True, mam. But I walking this night time because Ah have no choice – two young boy pickni, and the father dead. Have to look work. Thank you for the water mam. Ah was real thirsty. God bless you.'

'So where in these parts you expect to find work? Time hard you know, and people here have to look out for themselves too.'

'I know that mam. But my cousin in Lucea send me a message say a lady down there looking a live-in maid, and she prefer somebody from outside the town, so I pack up and I come. But dark catch me on the road so Ah say to meself mek Ah pray and stop at this nice-looking house, it look like is nice people live there.'

'Hnn. But your mouth sweet bad. You better watch how you use up that sweet mouth for it can get you in trouble, for a young girl. Hnn.'

My Uncle Cuthbert – Cuttie for short – had been in his young days just such a traveller. It was how he gleaned his magnificent stories, tales he told us that no one rivalled. Stories not like my mother's which were not real stories but stories about her childhood and growing up. Uncle Cuttie told us his own adventures but still they felt and sounded as if they were real, like stories in books about witches and fairies and gingerbread men and troll people and wolves. But his were stories about rolling calves and three-foot horses and whooping boys, and duppies with no feet and teeth like monsters, that attacked him at dead of night travelling the dark lonely roads so that he had to stoop down in the road and draw a circle with a cross on the top. It stopped the duppy in its tracks for when it saw a circle and a cross it could not cross over. Such stories happened only when you travelled at dead of night, alongside graves and cotton trees on hushed, moonless roads.

It was how Long Man came to us. Long Man was a man who seemed to have no people, no city and no wounds. I always thought of him as something like an eel – he lived not in places but in the spaces in between, and even when he stopped with us for days on end I never imaged him sitting still or jelling into the specific shapes into which people jell when they put down roots or otherwise become real. One minute he was not there, and the next he would be standing in our yard looking up at the sky and saying to my mother in his rough, grunting way, 'Going rain, Ionie', and I would see only his shadow, the shadow of an excessively long red man cast hologrammatically between me and the sun, floating slightly atop trees and bushes along highways and bemused country roads. Even his redness, a deep bright redness like bauxite earth, which should have made him a solid presence, seemed to me to be liquid, poured out, flowing and unflowing like the plasmic swell of a river overhung by trees.

He lived in the indeterminate space between the highroads and unexpecting shelters, sleeping wherever night found him, whether under the stars or under a well-known roof such as my mother's, where he would appear out of the blue and without warning at any odd time of day or year. He came with his crocus bag slung over his shoulder, a dark red ghost looming up out of the shadows behind her shoulder where she bent over, washing clothes or hoeing peas in the outjut of rock above our house.

'You frighten me, Long Man,' she would say, and he replied, 'Ionie, you too careless. You must learn to watch your back.' He strode into the house to drop his crocus bag behind the door where it would stay all day while he sat and smoked his jackass rope pipe and talked to her while she worked.

He never offered to help. But she seemed not to mind. She seemed to come alive, somehow, when he was around, as if a light had gone on inside her, the switch flipped by an invisible hand, its only evidence the sudden glow in her face and her raised voice singing, taking off like slim birds over the roofs and treetops. I never tired of hearing my mother singing – I thought it was the most beautiful thing in the world – clear and cold and fiery as ice. I loved Long Man's coming. Even though his presence faintly disturbed me, I loved Long Man's coming, because when he was there, all day my mother sang.

She trembled on the edge of a knowledge I could not share, you could see it in the way her whole body ruffled, like calling hens, even the plaits of her hair seeming to stand on end in the electrified light. This I could not name, but instinctively I felt him stand between my mother and me, and for this reason I dreaded him. This and the fact that he

107

was so tall and so large, so that I couldn't see the top or the contours of him, even when I stood on tiptoe and looked up in his face. He smelt of bush and fresh sweat and old sweat and dark earth, not the sort of earth you wanted to run out and eat when it rained, when the first patter of raindrops fell scabbing its skin, but the sort that lay black and clayey under thick bush by low-lying rivers. Yet he smelt like outside and faraway places, places that were open and without undergrowth. His smell was like the special smell that people and suitcases had when they had come from oversea, only in a different way.

When he came, when I was very small, I used to run to my mother and hug her legs tight tight, as tight as I could, as if with my arms' slight force I could stop her looking at him. But in this war of possession he always defeated me, for she could see him over my shoulders, far above where my arms could reach. When he swung me up in his arms and hoisted me on his shoulder so I could see the pigmy world from a great height, I felt both exhilarated and offended – exhilarated because of the terror and the grandeur of the threat of falling and the wide world's sweep, and offended because this was my father's place, his shoulder was where my father hoisted me every evening when I ran out screaming to meet him coming home from work, and where he carried me the long way to the clinic when I was sick and needed injections. Once coming back, bleeding and wounded from the injection, my hat, a bright pink one with roses and ribbons, fell off on a dog's carcass lying in the street. I was so horrified I didn't tell my father until we had gone very far from the dog, and each step we took my throat closed up further with silence because I didn't want my father to be angry with me for not telling sooner. When eventually I

108

whispered it in his ear, my father said, 'So why you didn't tell me before? Look how long we have to walk back now, and you sick', and we went back and found the dog and the bonnet and my father said we have to leave it because it drop on the dog, and I cried. I thought, thank God it was walking we were walking and not driving in a bus, for when you drove in a bus it made the people and the houses and the trees swim away, so that when the bus stopped people would find themselves in the wrong place, lost long miles from home, and their houses lost.

When my father came I looked at him closely to see if he was upset to see Long Man, but he never was: in fact they got on quite well, and that helped somehow to assuage my disquiet and my unknown rage.

Sometimes he stayed for just an afternoon, telling his stories, then he would get up in the sudden, abrupt way he had, swing his crocus bag over his shoulder and say, 'Well, Ionie, well, Barber, I gone again. Next time.' Led by our mother, we followed him to the gate and watched him melt away into the dark that, eel-like, swallowed him. He slid easily into the night as a knife through butter, smooth and silent and glidingly belonging. You felt the night was his home.

Sometimes he stayed longer, a weekend, resting his bones from the brukback work on Busha property, he said. Other times he stayed weeks, when there was work going on the DeLisser property at Point or the Briscoe one at Grant Ridge. He slid in and out of our presence and our routines as if he wasn't really there – I never remembered him disrupting anything. He stayed with us for a while but he didn't belong with us. He didn't belong to us. Or to any place. He never made a dent in anything he sat on, large though he was. He wore the same clothes all the time except for the one change he kept in his crocus bag, just in case he took sick and had to be taken to the hospital, he said. For such a careless man, he was extraordinarily superstitious about one day having to go to hospital. Sometimes he took off the tattered shirt and pants he wore and stayed in his long dirty underpants while my mother washed and bleached the outer clothes and spread them in the sun to dry.

My mother said he worked to earn enough money to feed himself and buy tobacco for an appointed time, and then he was on the move again. He never worked because the work was there or because the job wasn't finished. He worked only to fulfil his immediate needs. If he ever had a wife or a woman, our house was not the place you would hear tell of such things. If we had asked, my mother would have said if you want to be woman before your time, dipping your mouth in bigpeople business, see the door there and see Nellie Green house there, is there all mouthamassy will have to go and live.

He brought with him the thrum of adventure and strangeness and the great mystery and the wild and woven smells of outside. When he came my brothers and sisters were riveted, lost. Light swept into the house when he came and left when he left, yet he was a man of shadows and unfocused edges, whose eel-like presence found its métier in the dark and in hints of scattered rain. Apart from his redness and his height, I don't remember what he looked like, so at sudden, startling intervals over the years after he stopped coming, I found myself inventing stories about him, tall tales and shapes that I hung on the hologrammatic tall man.

His eyes were wild and colourless like water, they always looked out and away and, like rippled surface, they seemed shallow and deep both at the same time. I used to feel myself shiver like a hand had passed over my grave, when I looked into his eyes, for his eyes were not there. His voice was low and gravelly like someone who had smoked too much tobacco and belonged to the buttersoft, threatening dark. He had a woman once, for May May who my mother took in when she was fourteen and turned up at our house from where she had been living so-so in all alone St Ann, was his daughter. He ate spinning his plate on the tips of his five forgers, like my Uncle Brenton who lived in England and who my mother said was a worthless person, you could tell by the way he held his plate on his five fingers.

None of this of course, is strictly true. I remember almost nothing of Long Man, except that he was one of that elusive species, a traveller, and that he came and went like the wind, from unseen sources, to unknown destinations, that he was tall and red and as resistant to memory as an eel that pushes into secret places and yet refuses to be held, and that one day, after what must have been years, he stopped coming to us altogether. I thought my mother would have been sad, but she wasn't. When the years stopped altogether sliding him out into our yard from behind their dark doors, my mother calmly said, 'I think Long Man must be dead', and my father agreed, and long after that, years perhaps, somebody confirmed that he had indeed died, suddenly and quietly, in a district in St Ann. I don't know if he died in the hospital, but somehow I don't think he went. I wonder sometimes what became of the extra suit of clothes. Obviously they must have buried him in it. If he was buried at all.

It is strange that Cudjoe Man should reopen memories of Long Man, for apart from the fact that Cudjoe Man too was a traveller, there wasn't anything that they had in common. Cudjoe Man was thick and solid like my father, but there the resemblance ended. Cudjoe Man had hair in his nostrils and all over his arms. Sometimes he went barefoot and his feet were broad and splayed and horny, with great big toes that gripped the ground. My father was serious. Cudjoe Man always laughed. When he laughed his teeth were large and bold, and somehow projected a sense of massive, libidinous delight. As if he knew some joke about you that was enormously entertaining and enormously ramifying to his sense of who he was, and any minute now he would tell the joke and everyone would be laughing at you.

Cudjoe Man came to Baltree district the way all the other travellers came, on foot, one night when dark caught him on the road and he stopped by Pappa Lazzy's house to beg shelter for the night. At that time Pappa Lazzy was living with Cherry Blackett in Green Town. Two months after his wife Miss Martha die, before the earth over her grave even set, Pappa Lazzy up and move in with Cherry and before you blink he have about four or five children with her, even though he already have nine or ten big ones with Miss Martha. The whole thing create one scandal because Pappa Lazzy was a district constable and a elder in the Church of God church where people don't wrap up with sin. Cherry was thirty years younger than Pappa Lazzy and fat and pretty, full of the devil's own guile, my mother said, a snare for the feet of the hunter and a noisome pestilence, set as a serpent at the heels of weak old men afraid of their own ageing faces leaking in the dark.

Pappa Lazzy, never quick to condemn or turn away others since he knew his own sore, gave Cudjoe Man a bed on the floor for the night, and the next morning Cudjoe Man went out to look for work on the Briscoe property at Grant Ridge. He got the work and two twos he was saying to

Pappa Lazzy, 'Pappa, Ah feel in my spirit this is a good place, and these people Ah find meself amongst is good people. Ah really feel Ah can mek a livin here.' He moved out of Pappa Lazzy's house into a two room he rented from Maas Baada on the far side of Green Town and that was where he set himself up.

People liked Cudjoe Man. He fit himself in and was helpful in the community, doing his share when yam planting time came round and all the men rallied to give this one and that one a day, turn by turn until all the yam hills were hoed and planted. He was a great and enthusiastic domino player, and on cricket Sundays he could be depended on to contribute a few respectable runs to this or that side at the oval at Mango Walk.

But there was a thing that made Cudjoe Man stand out.

Cudjoe Man had a daughter. At the time they came to Baltree district Cudjoe Man said she was fifteen years old. But you couldn't really guess from the way she looked. She looked much younger. Her face was smooth like newly-bought paper, and her eyes slanted up at the corners like mine would if I pressed back the skin at the sides with my middle fingers. She was short and squat and bull-headed like her father; in fact as my sister Everette would have said if she was born then and the time was now, Cudjoe Man's daughter looked so much like her father, it was like she had Xeroxed him. In our district, children were supposed to look like their fathers. If a man was not sure whether a child imputed to him was his in truth, all he had to do was wait till it was born, then he would bring his relations to look at the child to see whether, if it didn't look exactly like him, it took after any family member from way back. Out of the mouth of these witnesses, based on physiognomy, a child's paternal fate was sealed. It was clear that Cudjoe Man's daughter's mother had been behaving herself and had not given Cudjoe Man jacket to wear.

Cudjoe Man worshipped the child. What made him strange and admired was that he looked after her like he was a woman. Until Cudjoe Man came, when people wanted an example to tell a proverb of how a man could worship his child, they talked of Miss Winnie husband George, who let it be known his daughter Angella was his piece of gold. Maas George had been known to go to the high school in Lucea with his machete looking for a boy who pushed his daughter one day on the bus. But after Cudjoe Man was like the year of our Lord – you could say, 'from Cudjoe Man and him daughter', the way people said, 'from Whappy kill Phillup', setting the timeline for every memorable experience that was the only one of its kind. The girl was neither pretty nor bright, in fact she was quite retarded, and this soon became clear even though every weekday morning Cudjoe Man dressing her up sleek and shining like new leather shoes and taking her himself in person to Miss Herfa school at Black Shop.

In fact on the first day after they settle in the district he personally take her to Miss Herfa herself and tell her, 'You see her here, teacher? She is me daughter, and I want you to take her in the school and put her in Six Book. She not the brightest, but she good and have manners, and she is fifteen this July coming, and I don't want her to keep back in any low class with any little pickni pickni for it not good for her age, it will make her feel small, and I don't want anybody not even my grandmother Casilda Isabella Campbell from March Pen St Catherine that grow me, to let my daughter feel small.'

According to Miss Nellie Green, post office Miss Clarice sister who know everything about everything, that is how Miss Zetta, who cook part time at the school and was in the school canteen kitchen wrapping salt when Cudjoe Man arrive with him daughter – according to Miss Nellie, that is how Miss Zetta say it happen, for Zetta she have ears all over her head and she hear everything, all what don't talk.

Quite taken aback, Miss Herfa sought to assure Cudjoe Man with caution that the school always did its best in the interests of the individual student, but they moved up by performance and not by age, so she couldn't really tell Cudjoe Man what 'book' to put his daughter in, she would have to test her and see. But Cudjoe Man insisted, and no one, not even Miss Nellie or Miss Zetta, knew by what method or by what means he got his way, for the girl can't spell bee from bull foot, in fact if she see her name on a bulla she would eat it all unconcerned, but get his way he did, and the girl get to sit in the Sixth Class in the All Age school. At Cudjoe Man's insistence, she get a seat in the front, and there she would sit, day in day out, the livelong day smiling sweetly at the teacher and everyone else in the room, hearing nothing and seeing nothing, but nodding her head every time the teacher ask a question, putting up her hand when all the other children put up theirs to show they know the answer to a question, smiling and nodding sweetly and saying, 'Yes teacher' the first day when the teacher thought she really meant it and called on her to answer. Her father sent her to school well equipped with crayons and drawing book, a luxury that few if any of the other parents felt they could afford. Cudjoe Man's daughter spent all her time doodling and crayoning long series of pothooks in these drawing books, with a masterful and prodigal liberality that took her through one book in

115

half a day. When the book was finished, she would go and stand up by the teacher's chair saying, 'Waan book, teacher', waiting patiently and refusing to move until the teacher get spook and grab a free issue exercise book from out the closet where the school hide away all the books the Government send down for the children to use, and put it open in front of her where she could see it had clean blank pages for her to draw on.

Just as Cudjoe Man said, she never made any trouble. She would just go back to her drawing, smiling and nodding and humming to herself. But always she would return the next day with a new drawing book from the endless store that Cudjoe Man seemed to spend his money procuring for her. 'Time Cudjoe Man done buy out all the drawing book dem inna Jamaica fi the likkle Fool-Fool, no odder else picket not going have nutten fi draw inna? Dem no going have to drop dat deh subject deh, or else order special shipment fi she?' Miss Nellie wanted to know.

If she had been more harmful, or her father more harmless, maybe the other children would have envied her. Some did try to borrow the luxurious crayons, either snatching them from under her hand without asking, or saying, 'Fool-Fool lend me you crayon', the perfunctory request and the snatching hand one smooth co-ordinated flow without a beat of separation between them. Little Fool-Fool allowed the lending without fuss, with that sweet, total smile so like her father's, but sometimes after she felt she had waited too long, and sometimes as soon as you borrowed the crayon and had started drawing, there she would be tapping you softly, softly on your shoulder, smiling sweetly and holding out her hand. 'Pencil. Want pencil. Mines.'

The first time a boy refuse to give back the crayon

(he just ignored her and went on drawing), Cudjoe Man's daughter get tired waiting, and she grab him by the shoulders and start to push. She push till the boy belly squeeze up against the desk edge and he start to gargle like he was going puke. It was a thing to see how the sad open smile give way to the tight concentration of rage, how her face screw up tight tight from the effort to dislodge the boy from his hold on her crayon. The whole thing cause one ruckus for in the end the bench on which two other children were sitting slide out from under them and everybody including Cudjoe Man's daughter fall in a tangle to the floor and Cudjoe Man daughter bust she head. The children start to laugh and the teacher get vex and punish everybody including Cudjoe Man daughter. The next morning, Cudjoe Man visit the school and carry on bad to Miss Herfa how the teacher punish him pickni for no reason at all and moreover cause her head to bust, and if was not that Miss Herfa herself was such a nice lady he woulda sue the school. Miss Herfa speak to him soft soft and apologize for the teacher, but before he leave, Cudjoe Man go out in the school yard where all the children could see him from the open doors of the open rectangle that was the school building, and raise up his fist that black and powerful like a cotton tree stump, and bawl out that any pickni that trouble him daughter if they think they bad, their parents better hide them good for if is even under the house bottom or the innermost bedroom he coming to haul them out from there and give them what they working for. Cudjoe Man sound and look terrifying, and for days after, nobody trouble Fool-Fool or borrow her crayon. After that the children find more subtle ways of hackling Fool-Fool, and though it get real dicey sometimes, Cudjoe Man never really have to come back to the school to warn anybody again.

117

Cudjoe Man's daughter even went to Friday school, to which only the idlest parents sent their children, especially in crop time when there was reaping to be done. Apart from the idle parents and Cudjoe Man, the only person who sent his child to Friday school was Maas George, whose daughter Angella was his piece of gold, she was bright bright like the morning star. Angella was another quiet one who however was a screamer – she screamed the whole district down if she was made to miss a day of school. She wore shoes and socks to school, not puss boot but real leather shoes, like a choice gift or special everyday sign, like tithes for the offering plate or the best part of the dinner laid by for your father before everybody else get to eat. Cudjoe Man's daughter didn't just wear shoes and socks, she owned and wore the most fantastic array of ribbons and clips, which despite her father's vigilance disappeared into other children's pockets and reappeared in their hair the next day, as fast as Cudjoe Man could replace them. Hair clips, like ribbons, are not easy to trace, carry no identifying mark to tell you they belong to one owner rather than another. Or at least so everyone thought. Cudjoe Man caught one of the thieves on her way from school one Thursday evening after he had put a secret mark on the ribbon so he could identify it, as he said, 'on any blasted fingersmith's head'. So then the ribbon and hair clip stealing eased down (though it don't exactly stop), and Cudjoe Man's daughter continued coming to school looking like a Christmas tree every single month of the year.

Big Man Cassells had a son named Lobi, who couldn't let a skirt pass by him untouched without serious personal distress because, as Miss Nellie put it, his purpose on earth was to let woman know that God send him on a special mission to furnish them with seed. One day this boy who was famous across three districts for his misbehaviours with women, cast his eye upon Cudjoe Man's daughter and said, 'But you know, is not a badlooking chick even though she not so pretty – she round and rosy and healthy like tomatis, matter of fact is the best kind of woman this, she can't answer you back and she can't ask you where you coming from and where you was last night.' Lobi was only joking, but that time was when people glimpsed the real deep-down Cudjoe Man that so far had only been coming out of the words of his mouth. Some people say the boy touch her and some people say he never touch her, he just cast his eye up and down her like he stripping something off. Whatever the case, Cudjoe Man wasn't asking any questions from nobody and that evening after he meet the boy at Black Shop, the boy go home leaving his two front teeth lying on the ground in front of Maas Tom liquor shop.

'Ah going sue you arse,' Big Man Cassells shout in Cudjoe Man face, pushing up his chest and brandishing his cutlass like flag in fronten red bull.

'Sue who? Sue who? Go get you blasted blue boot and come mek Ah climb eleven step wid you backside. Mek Ah put you before the judge fi slander and definition of character. You tink Ah don't hear how you pass remarks bout me and me daughter and what you tink I do with her? You tink bush don't got ears? An you tink me and you is one? Man, Ah want to respect you mother for she is a dead woman that never troble me, so try don't mek I tell you who do what with who. Man, move you arse outa me face fore I move it for you.'

Big Man Cassells didn't sue Cudjoe Man. People said he was afraid Cudjoe Man would win the case, for was common knowledge that Big Man Cassells had said in Miss Nellie's hearing that he didn't know what Cudjoe Man expected, didn't he think man had eyes to look, it look like Cudjoe Man want the girl for himself, and he personally wouldn't be surprise if things go on behind door in the dark that can't come to daylight. Big Man Cassells needed nobody to tell him that if he ever sue Cudjoe Man dog nyam him supper, for what Miss Nellie ears hear her mouth not kibbering, and what she don't remember she invent, and what not sweet enough she embroider. Is a brave man go take on Miss Nellie in front any judge, and Miss Nellie done declare say she willing to testify in court on Cudjoe Man behalf. Is how he coulda unravel that Anancy web? Furthermore she let it be known that nobody would give evidence for Big Man Cassells, because all the women were on Cudjoe Man's side, they were so impressed by the way he took care of his daughter. In the end it all worked out to the boy's advantage, because his father bought him two brand-new gold teeth, and he went about smiling frequently, opening his mouth wide so people could see the wealth within.

People asked, 'So Cudjoe Man why you don't married so you can have somebody to look after the child? Man can't look after girl child, you know, especially when they reach that age.'

'Reach that age? Reach that age?' Cudjoe Man say. 'You know how many years I looking after this girl child till she reach this age that you can now tell me bout reaching age? Elm, you know how long I looking after her? From the day the mother realize the child not bright like how she did dream, and she get up one morning and leave her in my hand, shame of the child even though her people they dunce like bat from all their generation, vex how the child don't wash out her curse.' Cudjoe Man flashed his eyes like rolling calf and smiled his wide, rabid smile. 'You see that girl? Is me is the only mother she know from the day she born and that is the way it going to stay.'

And he explained that he would never marry for he don't want any woman bad treating or advantaging his child. Everybody knew by this time that Cudjoe Man visiting by Miss Zetta second daughter Dottie, but Cudjoe Man never take her into his house and he and she don't have any children, so is as if all his attention give to the little Fool-Fool.

The district had named her this name of its own decision. It was the kind of household nickname, given without judgement or pity, by which they called anyone who was not totally there in the head. Her real name was Dolly. Her father called her Doll-Doll.

Cudjoe Man took the girl everywhere with him – to cricket, to Saturday market in Maaga Bay square, to fair and donkey race.

She walked beside him in her neat clean clothes and Christmastree-hair that Cudjoe Man combed, holding tightly to her father's hand, nodding to herself and smiling that wide clown's smile that was half her father's smile and half something else that belonged to her alone. Nobody really knew the extent of her isolation from the normal world, since she spoke so little, but Cudjoe Man said she could clean and wash, and iron without burning herself, and as a matter of fact was she who washed her own clothes and kept the house clean, he said. Cudjoe Man's house was spotlessly clean, as were his clothes. Nobody really believed him.

He was very proud of her.

Watching them walking side by side you couldn't figure who was prouder of whom, the two of them smiling foolishly and Cudjoe Man holding conversation as if he really thought she understood. They held curious talks with the neighbours, odd three-cornered dialogues in which Cudjoe Man addressed his answers to his neighbours not directly to them but through his daughter, a quirky ventriloquism that encircled her in an ordinary, everyday world.

'Doll-Doll, you want grater cake and fritters? Yes, Miss Lilla, sell me two grater cake and two fritters deh, nuh?'

'The little one looking well today though, Cudjoe Man. You take good care of her bad.'

'Yes, man, is the one, you know, don't know if I go get no more, so haffi take care, eh Doll? Plenty man don't get any, what you say? How the fritters taste? Nice, eh? Nice, nice. She love a fritter you see Miss Lill, love a fritter you bawl.'

And all the time is the little Fool-Fool he looking at, like she is a medium or a conduit that he expect to take water or the dead to the other side.

'Cudjoe Man you and the likkle one walking out though,' Miss Nellie shouting out from her front verandah where she watching people business and taking the evening breeze in the cool just before dusk up, when all the delicate blooms and scents of night flowers coming out and Cudjoe Man and little FoolFool walking out among them hand in hand, their heads framed up among the bloom of stars.

'Evenin, Miss Nellie, evenin, Pappa Lazzy. Yes, jus taking a likkle breeze out nuh, ehn Doll? Say evening to the big people nuh, Doll?'

'Evenin, Miss Nellie, evenin, Pappa Lazzy,' little Fool-Fool nods and sheds her beaming smile on all the world. 'Taking a likkle breeze out.'

'Yes, dear heart. Nice, nice. Enjoy youself now.'

'Yes, enjoy meself.' Her voice takes on the tone and rhythm of Miss Nellie's, a perfect, unconscious mimicry, smoother than tracing paper filled out over a map.

◆

Cudjoe Man and his daughter sitting on Arawak Wall out by Black Shop and the father telling the daughter ancient history like he think she sitting for Jamaica Third Year. Cudjoe Man answering for he and she in one, the little Fool-Fool only nodding and smiling and looking up in his face.

'You remember how Ah tell you it last time, Doll? Yes, man, of course I know you remember, then don't I know you have good brain? Dem-was a peaceful people that don't trouble nobody, just like you and me, Papa, unless somebody trouble dem. They eat cassava and corn and anything else they plant with they own hand in God good earth, and they eat the fish that swim in a hundred river, up and down this land. Is them name this place you know, Xaymaca, but the white people mix it up and call it Jamaica, for they can't pronounce it so good. I remember, Papa, but what it mean again? Land of wood and river, yes Papa I member, I member now! Evenin, Missa Bollo, yes, me an the girl chile tekkin a breeze. Howdy Minna, bwoy, girl, what a way you look good in the evening here now, why you so stiffnecked girl, why you keep running from progress? Look how long I want to married to you, and you putting me off?'

'Walk 'way, Cudioe Bwoy, married to who? You think you can mind woman like me? You don't see say I come off a high table? Evenin, Dolly. Is what you filling up the girl child head with again now? You don't see the child tired of you?'

'Is so you think. Come ask her and see how she larn you you history. What this girl know they don't teach you in school, ehn, Doll? But is awright, gwan you ways. One of these days Samson go lef you backside, and who you go run come to that time? You go beg me fi tek you.'

'Heh! Keep on a wait! Eat you heart out!'

'Eat my heart out? Heh, congotay!'

'Heh! Congotay!' Minna, a round, buxom girl with dancing eyes and flirtatious buttocks, mocks him with her mimicry, but she is genuinely curious, wondering what he and the child talking about so close. It is a part of the flirting, which she loves to death, but gets to practise only the few times she can escape Samson's vigilant eye, which is as swift and turbulent as his rage.

'So mek me hear the history lesson then nuh? See what you foolin up the chile bout this time.'

She lingers, as much to delay arriving home as to spread herself in the warm grace and boldness of his eye. She carries a water bucket on her head, balanced liltingly on a bright plaid cotta that allows it to sway from side to side without falling. Their banter is an established pattern, the rules and the boundaries known to both, tacitly accepted, yet delicate as Anancy's web, for they both know that if she lifts the rules' gossamer even for a moment, he will not hesitate to seize the gift proffered, and she – she is poised on the edge of accepting. She knows it in the quick heat running between her thighs, for in her eyes he is a comely man, dark and hard as steel and banked, warm, tumid rain. Their eyes meet with a knowing, secret as furled roses, and he breaks the tension, linking eyes with his daughter.

'Ha! So you think me no know wha me a chat say, eh? Dolly, mek she hear we now. Tell her bout Columbus. Tell her how he come with a whole set o' other white people and kill out the Arawak dem. How they dry up plenty river and nearly drink the sea. Only lef two pretty girl like you and she.'

'Like you and she,' Doll-Doll obediently repeats, smiling sweetly at Minna, her sweet, open sad smile like a weeping clown's. Her mimic's talent is startling, exquisite.

Minna laughs, the warm round sound gurgling the air like water. Her head is thrown back, exposing the dark chocolate of her throat, the quick rise and fall of the chocolate silk of her breasts smoothly hillocking the long slope.

'What a set a idiot you be,' she cries. Her speaking breath intersects the rapid rise and fall, pants through her open lips. 'You is a real ole idiot!' she cries, scornful and approving, charmed.

Cudjoe Man's voice rasps like harsh wire in his throat. He catches her fiercely by the wrist, consciously hurting her. 'You know girl, you give me serious trouble in here so you know.' His other hand hits his chest in a gesture too harsh to be melodramatic. 'If was not for this likkle girl standin here wid me you see – is she save you you know. Is she save you.'

She cries out half in quick anger, half in the pain that has engendered the anger. 'So what you coulda do me, Cudjoe Man? What you coulda do me if the likkle girl was'n here? Is what you think you coulda do me?'

He bares his teeth in a sudden threat that sizzles the air with their passion, all play burnt clean. 'You want me tell you? You really want me tell you?' He advances purposefully on her, pelvis thrust forward in an exaggerated pose of male aggression that startles her with sudden fear; she gasps, pulls her hand savagely through his, and flees down the road, water bucket tilted precariously on her cotta. He watches her go, the water splashing over the sides of the rocking pan, and he doesn't see the water but imagines the wetness and the sharp succulent rise of her nipples against the dark cloth where it has spilled.

'Come on, Dolly,' he growls, grabbing her hand, and then, more softly, as he watches the dawning bewilderment and loss in the wide open eyes, 'come on, sweets, mek we go home.'

'Yes, Papa. Night a come.'

'True, sweets, night a come.'

◆

Trouble with Samson was bound to come, Miss Nellie say, leaning over her gate and talking to the world at large. Samson was a man known in the district for his savage temper and his rabid jealousy over Minna. Nobody could look at the girl without he accusing them of either wanting to turn her gainst him, if was a woman, or putting question to her, if was a man. People have it to say he use to beat up the girl too, any time him temper rise gainst some man that he fraid to beat up for he don't have any real evidence except that Minna as usual too quick with her smile, that smile that always seem to betray her for it pop out of her lighting up she face and the whole world round her whether she will or no, once she see another human being fronten her. Was like Minna couldn't really help herself – the girl born to smile, born with a smile inside her like is pure sun and immortelle and river singing was going on when her mammy and pappy was making her, and the whole thing make a soup and go inside Minna bone and just stream out in her heart and her smile – the girl have a heart and a smile too big for her body to hold in, no matter how hard she try – and she really try, just so as not to provoke that damn ass piece a darkness Samson Culley, damn fool and dark like all the rest of Mango Walk peopledem, can't read nor write, dark as middle night. I keep saying nothing from Mango Walk no good, and see it there, Samson Culley prove it when he take the woman good good pretty pretty pickni try turn her into toofenkeh. You ever hear anybody try to kill smile – you don't see something wrong with the man, eh?

I never really hear or see any of the beating for myself, but I believe it, Miss Nellie say, for is not Zetta Murray alone testify to it, plenty Maaga Bay people who go to the Church of God church use to talk about it, and sometimes I notice the girl have bruise under her neck and she wear her tie-head way down over her eye like she hiding something. It grieve me heart till Ah cyaan tell you how, for everybody love Minna, that girl so nice, she wouldn't hurt a fly. You know, I always say to myself she drawn to Cudjoe Man and that little Fool-Fool because them is the same kinda people like she – love laugh. You ever notice how Cudjoe Man smile and how that little girl laugh light up her whole face – though to tell gospel truth sometime you feel her laugh not so right – like it coming out from some dark root where laugh and cry melt up together or never even really separate so they don't really have any meaning – but no so, that cyaan surprise you, for no must be somewhere so in a dark confuse place fool-fool people live? Poor, poor likkle thing.

You see me, Nellie Green, Miss Nellie say, I is not one to watch people business like Zetta Murray, but is long time I noticing the vibe between Cudjoe Man and Minna, and I coulda tell you from far back that troble brewing, for when tongue an teeth meet, who can come between? I know the girl couldn't really have any love for Samson, and is not me one in the district sure that Samson tie her, visit Butty Cassells obeahyard and tie her, for every time the girl try to lef, she cyaan lef. Every work she get, he either go there go tell lie on her so the peopledem come to distrust her and ask her to leave, or he fake heart attack and all sort of sickness so she

127

haffi run lef her job come back home. I hear he even follow her to bathroom to see if she have man hide under her skirt or if she throwing away something from between her legs that he don't and can't put there. He beating her up because he lose his nature long time and can't even give her a child – beatin her up say is her fault why they don't have any, say she give him bad bush kill him nature. Damn darkness. What Minna put up with, nice nice pretty pretty black girl, I don't know how she don't lose her smile. But I know troble was a brew from the day I look through that window on the Maaga Bay side and see her playing with Cudjoe Man sitting on that Arawak Wall. Ah say to meself, see troble here, something and something meet.

In the end, it was not Samson but Miss Zetta's second daughter Dottie who set the match that set the whole house ablaze. Cudjoe Man started keeping company with Dottie some time after he arrived in the district. Visiting and providing for her, but he didn't take her to live with him in the house he rented from Cherry's father, Maas Baada Blackett. Dottie was nothing like Minna, either in looks or personality. Minna was effervescent where Dottie was quiet. Minna was round and luscious and creamy like chocolate on lollipop sticks, her smile trapped sunlight, her laugh the gurgle of running water, constant and free and plentiful like Morris Hole River in the summers when school and children were out. Dottie was plain and light-skinned with a long, slightly stupid face like a picture of a sheep, and when she spoke her voice was low and gentle and kind, not a spear of silver cleaving the wind. Everyone liked Dottie, both for herself and because she was not stuck up like her sister Merdel who everyone called The Dryland Tourist because though she had never gone over sea, she walked as if her foot disdained the ground, and talked only to say 'Good morning' and 'Good evening' in a clipped, English kind of voice while looking over your head into the heart of beautiful things which you were not good enough to see. Merdel had education, Dottie did not. Dottie went to church and read her Bible and was courteous and kind to everyone. She couldn't hurt a fly.

But one evening Dottie met Minna coming from the standpipe with her water bucket on her bright cotta, singing and calling out, 'Hi Dottie girl, how things?'

'Don't Dottie girl me, you man-tiefin likkle hypocrite,' Dottie give out, and she fetch Minna a box that fly the bucket off her head and wet up both of them and would have chopped off Minna's foot if she hadn't caught it in time, mid-air before it fell to the ground. Dottie nearly win the fight for she catch Minna so much by surprise – she get in a couple good licks before Minna recover herself and start giving better than she get, for underneath that supple chocolate skin Minna strong like bull cow – but how else you think she withstand the kind of blows a man like Samson Culley could deliver? Two twos a big crowd gather, some really horrified and crying out for shame and disgrace, others enjoying themselves hugely, is only the drum they waiting for to beat like carnival – 'Yes Minna gal, lick her, lick her good!'

'Dottie, gal, show you fist!' In the end it was Pappa Lazzy and one of the respectable elders from the Church of God church that come along and part the fight. They had to give Dottie Miss Nellie apron to cover herself because when they haul Minna off her her whole skin expose for her dress was in shreds and her underwear showing. Blood streaming thin from the corner of her mouth where she dainty spit out a tooth. Minna lose the skin over one eye and get a little bite up bite up and bruise up bruise up.

I was very sad because I liked Dottie and Minna both, and it hurt me to think of them being enemies and what would I do if, as often happened, I met them both on the road at the same time. Which side was I supposed to take? Was I to say, 'Good evening, Miss Minna' turning my face ashamedly to the right, and then, 'Good evening, Miss Dottie' turning to my left? I decided that perhaps I would say good evening very fast and walk on looking neither to the right nor to the left, not giving either of them a chance to make jokes with me the way they used to before the fight, for I didn't want to let either of them feel bad on account of me. There was no one to ask advice because this was not picknibusiness, this was bigpeople story.

◆

The thing that hurt Samson most of all wasn't that Dottie fight Minna, but that in fighting Minna, Dottie had declared to all of Baltree district that he was no man at all. She show everybody clear as daylight that he was getting bun. Up to then, his own suspicions had been all his witness, insistent, garrulous but unreliable whisperers, stealers of a man's dreams that creep into his house between shadow and waking, sharp and silver dark and imaginary as leaves in moonlight after a hard November rain. When you woke up in the morning, the leaves and the trees on which they stood were solid and real, neither moon nor shadow had carried them away; and for another precious small parcel of moments, you could wrap up another packet of dreams, holding them close in your fist against the moon and sleeping and the night. But Dottie fighting had shattered all that – shattered all possibility of recovered dream, and all possibility of waking. Dottie was no tegereg and no brawler – she was milder than the sea at dawning or the heart of flowers before they are opened. If Dottie fought, she had just cause. She knew the truth. She had gone into Samson's heart and drawn the whisperers out by the red red wrists, and ushered them into open court. The district would have to judge.

That night Samson beat Minna until her screaming woke the district from Green Town to Maaga Bay and he lost control of his own voice. The children awoke from their slumbers in terror from his hoarse, anguished roaring like a kennelled lion I heard years later at Hope Zoo where it cried itself to death after years in captivity and isolation. The adults shushed them hastily back to bed – but not to sleep – and, armed with flashlights and bottle torches, descended upon Samson's house where they had to drag him off Minna by knocking him down with a slat of board which Pappa Lazzy had, with preternatural presence of mind, torn from his abandoned outside kitchen at the last minute before he ran out of the yard, calling for help.

Minna was unrecognizable. Her plump, pretty face had disappeared under ribbons of blood like somebody had hung crimson cloth on a clothesline and cut it with scissors, little by little, into thin streamers for a festival parade. Her dress too was in tatters and it and her whole body were drenched in something dark that could have been sweat or blood or even kerosene, of which there was a strong odour in the room's thick violent air. Her breasts were exposed as if someone had hated them, for her dress over them was wrung to one side and ripped, the cloth gaping with a violent aliveness, as if somehow the rage in the hands that had seized it had imprinted itself on the inanimate cloth for ever, and the whole web and waft was instinct with the feeling. Somebody, one of the women, bending with quick tenderness, put a white lace scarf around her, like a bride. Her eyes were closed, and she didn't say anything. But you could see her breathing, faint and low, her chest rising and falling beneath the grotesque costume of blood, or sweat, or kerosene.

'Jesus Christ. Jesus Christ Almighty', Maas George kept saying over and over again, like a man in a dream, and for once Miss Winnie didn't have the heart to tell him to stop taking the Lord's name in vain. The litany was a grateful noise, holding everyone pendent in a hung bubble of sanity, desperately clutched before it broke.

Samson lay on the floor, bleeding from the head wound from Pappa Lazzy's lath, but fully conscious. A terrible sound came from him, an anguished, hopeless moaning that seemed to come from beyond the reaches of what was human, from some dark, forgotten place to which only the ends of experience could return a man.

The bubble broke. 'Shut you noise, man!' Maas Bollo Rajjo broke out, his voice rising. 'What the blast you there moaning and groaning for, after you try kill the woman. You is a man?'

Everyone was silent, for the same thought seized each imagination – was this on the floor beast or man? The sound was like no human sound, yet what beast could summon up this agony of suffering, this wild disintegration of sound from beyond the corridors of speech, where noise, and noise alone was enough, pure and nascent as rage?

'A wheh Levi deh with the car, man? Why him no hurry up? We haffi tek the girl to the hospital quick quick fore she dead pon we.' The practicality galvanized the crowd into

132

renewed action. The atmosphere of prayer broke; people broke out into renewed excitement, shouting orders, giving instructions, cursing, praising God, ritualizing the night's events into liveable noise. A brief scuffle, a commotion outside, a voice raised above the din, 'Move outa me way, Ah seh. Mek me pass.'

The voice, deadly and powerful, raised yet curiously quiet, was Cudjoe Man's. One of the boys at the door cried out, his voice high as a girl's with apprehension and fear. 'Maas Bollo, Maas Bollo, don't mek Cudjoe Man get inside! Him have a machete!'

◆

I don't know how it really happened that night because there was so much excitement and so many people had their side of the story to tell, as you can see from all the interruptions that come in from I start to tell you the story until now. Nothing like this had ever happened in our district before, though you heard of it happening in other places, so distant and so far away in time that people spoke of it in proverbs, like the time Whappy kill Phillup and it was his last killing for ever because after that he went to the gallows. The most I, a child, who was therefore never directly addressed and was not encouraged to ask questions about bigpeople business – the most I could make out that seemed for sure, was that when Cudjoe Man broke loose from the men at the door and rushed inside the room with his cutlass, he didn't go straight for Samson as people were terrified he would. 'Cudjoe Man, Cudjoe Man,' Pappa Lazzy called out, tears flowing down his voice, 'Ah beg you do, don't shed any more blood here tonight. The district can't take any more blood tonight.'

Cudjoe Man ignored him, dropping the cutlass and instead going down on his knees beside Minna on the floor. He take her head and shoulders in his arms gentle as a child, people say, and he hold her up against his chest saying over and over again like Maas Bollo, 'Jesus Christ, Jesus Christ, Jesus Christ', and then he start to cry.

Some people say he wait until Maas Levi car come and take out Minna, and some say he cry and cry until he can't cry no more and then he put down Minna gentle as a babe and grab him cutlass, and some say is Samson fast attack him when he see him hold up Minna, which go to show that all that moaning and bawling on the floor was one big pretence to gain people sympathy.

◆

Miss Nellie leaning over her fence post telling everybody that passing by, 'But you know, life is so unfair. Same thing I was saying to Idalyn up to yesterday. I feel for a fact Cudjoe Man never take Minna, he take Dottie instead because deep down he fraid Minna come between him and the child. Is plenty time I looking at them through the window on the Maaga Bay side, you know I don't really watch people business but that window open out on everything under the sun and even when you turn you eye away to avoid seein what you not suppose to see, things come to you vision so fast you don't have time to even kibber you eye. Plenty time I seein them when they playin, you know how young people play they play when they in likes, they throw word like is hide and seek, and sometime he watchin her, Cudjoe Man watchin Minna with that look in him eye, watchin her watchin the likkle girl like him tryin to find out the answer to a question or some form of riddle. Always watchin her with that question in him eye, but it never quiet, like he never find the answer.'

◆

After Cudjoe Man went to jail, Little Fool-Fool went to live with Miss Winnie and Maas George and Angella and their other six children for a while. She kept on going to Miss Herfa school at Black Shop, carrying her bright red school bag with the drawing book and crayons. Her hair was still neat but not so pretty pretty because Miss Winnie had four girl children's hair to comb for school in the mornings, and it takes time to put in all those ribbons and clips. But after a short while Cudjoe Man's people from St Catherine came and took Little Fool-Fool away. That was the first time I really understood that Cudjoe Man had relatives. They came one Thursday after the sun was going down and we had already come home from school and done our chores and were stealing as much play time as we could before we got called in for the night.

'Look, look!' my brother Linval said, and he pointed out to where a black Austin Cambridge car drew up at Maas George and Miss Winnie gate and a tall fat woman in a hobble skirt and spike heels, and a short wide man looking like Cudjoe Man got out and knocked at the gate. We drew near, hushed with curiosity, and watched as Miss Winnie came out in answer to their knock. She didn't ask a lot of questions so you could tell she was expecting them. We watched as they went inside and after a time they came out again holding Little Fool-Fool by the arms between them, one on her right and the other on her left, like thief that crucify. The man was carrying a dulcimina in his other hand and the woman carried a BOAC travelling bag. Miss Winnie followed with a cardboard box. Little Fool-Fool was wearing a bright red dress and her hair was looking all over like a Christmas tree again, with all her clips and red ribbons like she was going on an outing. We crowded to the fence and watched them put the things in the back of the car, and then Little Fool-Fool climbed in and the woman shut the door, and then the man and the woman got in the front seat and they drove away. Little Fool-Fool knelt up on the back seat, staring out at us as she drove away. I felt uneasily that something was required of us so I lifted my hand and waved. My brothers also lifted their hands and waved. Little Fool-Fool kept staring at us until she almost couldn't see us any more, and then she too lifted her hand and waved. It struck me only long afterwards why she looked so strange – she wasn't smiling, that wide greedy smile that was like her father and something else that was completely her own, that I couldn't name.

◆

And it's the way Little Fool-Fool slides out the buried back of my mind in a picture of that day with her hair oiled and bright with red ribbons, that brings the pattern back from behind where it hiding like when wins wiss cover over door that stop use long time because the house abandon. My inside eye bend back the way thread bend back over a thimble when you crocheting backstitch and I see over the red dust of the falling evening Long Man rolling up to our front gate little bit after Cudjoe Man leave us, and then was the last time I ever see him for this time when he move on again after about two weeks sitting there in our front yard smoking his jackass rope tobacco and making my mother sing, the doors of the years close quietly behind him and we never see Long Man again. The years swallow him up just like how they swallow Cudjoe Man, jus like how when you move a house because you travelling the brown and red earth fill in after a while because sun shine and rain fall and the house spot tired waiting in case the native change him mind and return.

But at that time I never really studying Long Man too much because the whole thing with Cudjoe Man affect me bad bad, my mother say, and I start having nightmare that my father drive off like Little Fool-Fool in the back of a black Austin Cambridge motor car and I never see him again. She feel that is because just around that time my father get a work in Somerton St James and didn't come home except on weekends for two whole weeks.

◆

Every evening when my father was due from work, I sat out on the fence post fronting our yard waiting for him to come home. No matter how my mother shouted and called, or said, 'Marlene, come in now nuh, you father not coming home for now, come get you dinner', or, 'Come wash you face.' No matter how the others called me for a last play under the daylight sky before we were forced inside for the night. After a while, they left me alone.

Nothing could call me away until I saw him form out of the clouds of the distance, as real as falling asleep warm, or red earth in clumps soiling the doorstep, telling you there was a man in the house and yes, there were the muddied waterboots in the corner by the door to prove it once and for all. A man who made dents on anything he sat on, because he was so real. More real than old wives' tales and black people gossip and old naygar goat mouth that said travellers sometimes never came back. And all during the time he was in Somerton St James I didn't stop looking out for him evenings, watching to see his tall head heaving towards me out of the mists and duppy smoke of the slippery time of day between sleeping and waking. I felt that just like any other evening, he would come home. I watched and willed and waited, keeping him alive by the skeins of stories I wove in my head, sacred as a book of prayers, bright scarves of stories in green and blue and red and gold and the soft grey light of afternoons when it rained and the whole sky over the sea was bright and tender like the soft inside of shells. Stories that were for warmth when I could not fall asleep. Stories hoisted about my father's shoulder where he swung me every evening when I ran out screaming to meet him coming home from work, and where he carried me the long way to the clinic when I was sick and needed injections. Once coming back, bleeding and wounded from the injection, my hat, a bright pink one with roses and ribbons, fell off on a dog's carcass lying in the street. I was so horrified I didn't tell my father until we had gone very far from the dog, and each step we took my throat closed up further with silence because I didn't want my father to be angry with me for not telling sooner. When eventually I whispered it in his ear, my father said, 'So why you didn't tell me before? Look how long we have to walk back now, and you sick', and we went back and found the dog and the bonnet. I thought, thank God it was walking we were walking and not driving in a bus, for when you drove in a bus it made the people and the houses and the trees swim away, so that when the bus stopped people would find themselves in the wrong place, lost long miles from home, and their houses lost. And I thought thank God I have my father, for though the people and the houses were lost, I was safe. And my father never got angry because I could not tell him how my bonnet fell off on the body of the dog.

My mother said she got really worried when I woke up crying because in my dream Little Fool-Fool knelt up on the back seat of the black Austin Cambridge her face looking like a new corpse with the smile just gone, and when I waved to her and she waved back her new corpse's face wavered before my eyes like a picture dropped in water and when the blur cleared it was my father lying in a hearse. My mother started making sure I didn't eat late because eating late made you dream, and she stayed up with me rubbing my stomach with healing oil she heated in her palms over the Home Sweet Home lamp and singing, 'Just Across on the Ever Green Shore' and 'Jesus Friend of Little Children' in her birdflight voice turned down low and crooning like the wick of newly trimmed lamps in the in-between spaces when you're saying good night and getting ready for bed and outside between the window slats you can see the shining stars.

Soon I stopped dreaming that dream, but one night I dreamed instead that my father had gone over the sea on a washed grey day when the sky was tender like the insides of shells. My father was not a fisherman but my Grampa Eric whom I hated and whose death had brought my first wake, used to be and stayed out late nights on end while, waiting, my mother and her sisters and brothers and her mother Chrisanna were afraid. In my dream they found the boat at sea and the body of the boy who went with my father to draw up the fish-pots, but they never found my father. They had a service in the Wesleyan church but I never went, I refused to go because my father was not dead. I hated my mother because she went, she betrayed him, she listened to the people who said, 'Poor fatherless. Poor poor fatherless. Once you don't find the body, it wash out to the horizon of the sea, into the mouth of sharks.' But afterwards I reconciled to my mother because she said, 'I didn't go because your father is dead, I go to say a prayer for him, wherever he is. Better always to pray in God house than by yourself alone.' And in my dream she let Long Man walk down the road, into the cloudy wind's embrace.

In my dream I fought the wind and the rain and the years' dark doors and hearses that were Chevrolets, and I kept my father's waterboots under the bed and looked at them all the time. They were the ones he should have worn to the fishing but changed his mind at last and wore his ordinary shoes instead. His waterboots had mud on them like they belonged to a man who was real and had taken them off only yesterday, a heart's beat away. And any minute now he would come through the door, calling, 'Marlene, Marlene, you see me waterboots?' and I would fly outside on wings to help him clean and put them back on, and he would hug me tight tight tight and swing me up so high I would see the horizon and touch the moon and the stars. And we would go laughing together out of the yard. This is what I dreamed.

And the next morning when I woke up it was so.

Later, much later, when I was more grown, I looked back over the years and thought about death and dying and loss and grieving and how some people went and some people stayed and how some made a noise when they went and some went so smoothly, so silently into the wind's embrace, and how lucky I was that my father stayed and that he left his dent on things that he sat on and touched. But that time all I was was happy because I was holding my father's hand and we were laughing as I went with him out into the open yard.

SO FEW AND SUCH MORNING SONGS

*... And nothing I cared, at my sky blue trades, that time
    allows*
In all his tuneful turning so few and such morning songs
Before the children green and golden
Follow him out of grace ...

Dylan Thomas, 'Fern Hill'

Bam! Bam! Baddam! Bam! Bam bam bam! Baddam bam!
Cho, arseness, lostness, blastness, hell. The morning sun
rises off the cusp of Breadnut Hill pale and pure as music
shafting the sky, and the sounds of Mister Papacita's
awakening, shrieking encounters wounding pots and pans
and broken bruised furnishings lance the sweet pure arc, a
perverse rainbow spattered with the rain of bile and spit in
the drunken corners of Mister Papacita's morning mouthfuls
of Massive from the night before, bile and spit like pooled
emissions from the strings of a broken heart leaking their
way around the edges of song with which every morning
below and above the cymballing broken pots and pans Mister
Papacita beats the sacrificial air, 'One a dese fine fine time!
one a dese fine fine time! Ah go bruk dung de house an go
'way! Ah go bruk dung de house an g'way!'

Mister Papacita bobs and weaves among the shambles
of his morning's handiwork trailing ribbons of blood
like incense where he has fumbled and failed to find his
one last pair of shoes among broken bottle fallen sullenly
with rage shamelessly scattering prodigal selves across
the weeping floor, weaves and bobs his baretoed way out
through the doorway of his prison stepping high and blind
onto the cold keen crabgrass that fronts his house like an

141

open floor, colder than polished glass with the sharpened dew. And though his song is fouled with the morning-after smell of drink and dreams, Mister Papacita is a master of syncopation, his singing's rainbow lances the swift intervals of the sun's fierce becoming as the knife lances an animal's throat making bright patternings on an altar. The sun's long leap streaks a paean of gold across the sky's sweet scroll and Mister Papacita howls his sickness to its sweep: 'One a dese fine fine time one a dese fine fine time!' Gold trembles on the edge of crimson, melts, flows into the greening heart of the morning's cymbals, the sky leaps with the crescendo of its carnival of flags. The glory opens out like an umbrella over Mister Papacita's despair, 'Bruk dung de house, bruk dung de house … AN G'WAY!', and folds it into itself, making a oneness of the earth and sky, laughter and weeping, music and howling, sun, sorry soil and stars.

In his sober moments, scattered like commas across the broken phrases of drink that had replaced the sentences of his life since his wife Miss Aita died, Mister Papacita was still the greatest singer that our district ever knew, greater even than my mother whose sudden wild shivers of song could skim the tops of the tallest trees, slimmer and purer than white birds in flight on green mornings, but who kept her singing hoarded to herself like miser's gold. Mister Papacita's voice was a giving more prodigal than wells and rivers, a deep bass thrum deeper and more plangent than a four-string guitar that graced our funerals, wakes and diggings like a gift of tongues.

It was to the children that he was the greatest grace of all. Who could have imagined up this carnival Don Quixote riding home from the killing fields slouched under the evening sun on the big-assed wall-eyed donkey named Vilma for the first girl he had loved, the long body, narrow and straight like a figure eleven, leaning in the saddle to the rhythm of her high-stepping dance, the curve-billed machete hanging across the pommel like a lance in rest as sighting us he slung the gauntlet of his voice to the glad air, joyously inviting us to the tournament of song, 'A who seh Sally dead? A who seh Sally dead, oh-ohi? Sing, sing, sing Sally, oh-ohi!' And joyfully we leaped to pick up the refrain, 'A who seh Sally dead? A who seh Sally dead, OO, OO? Sing, sing, sing, Sally OO, OO!' Laughing and singing as we skipped in the loud road circling Mister Papacita like pigeons circling tourists scattering crumbs or children circling their father for a morsel of his special man-of-the-house dinner even though they have already eaten their own.

'One nadda time Mister Papacita one nadda time!' So Mister Papacita throws us the chorus another time, 'A who seh Sally dead, OO, OO? A who seh Sally dead, OO, OO!' And we, perverse, well versed in the arts of tournament, discard the opening courtesies for open war, 'A me seh Sally dead, OO! OO! A me seh Sally dead, OO! OO!' Running shrieking with laughter and joy between Mister Papacita's legs in and out beneath and around the donkey's belly we pretended to allow ourselves to be easily caught, and always one was bound to be so that the game could go on. The prisoner of war hung upside down across Mister Papacita's donkey's pommel, mock-pummelled by Mister Papacita's flying fist, 'Cry cree! Cry cree!' 'No, bwoy, don't cry cree! Don't cry cree!' we scream in support of the necessary prisoner, our hapless ally, but finally the culprit gives in, 'Me seh Sally no dead, OO! OO! Me seh Sally no dead, OO! OO!' and the rest of us, derisive, chant in counterpoint, 'Yu wrang! Yu wrang! Yu wrang fa Sally dead, woie-oie!' Mister Papacita cracks the donkey's rope left right and centre, and we flee half-routed down the broken road throwing over our shoulders our defiant, gleeful challenge, 'Yu wrang! Yu wrang! Yu wrang fa Sally dead, woie-oie!' but Mister Papacita's voice outsoars ours, 'A who seh Sally dead, e-hn, e-hn? A who seh Sally dead, e-hn, e-hn?'

Always, it was the splendour of Mister Papacita's singing voice, round and rich and resonant as a bass organ primed with rum, that defeated us.

Our mothers struggled to wean us from Mister Papacita's ribald songs, whose ribaldry we discovered only after we were grown:

> O Ah tell you bout a man name Willie
> O Ah tell you bout a girl name Sue
> If Ah tell you bout de way dem kill i'
> What is dat to you?

This was Mister Papacita's favourite morning hymn. Every morning it rises in oblation with the steam from Miss Aita's coalpot carrying the smell of boiling chocolate like incense across the doorways of the neighbours' houses. My brother Tony, eager as an acolyte, pops his two suck fingers out of his mouth and opens it wide to sing Mister Papacita's songs, 'Oh Ah tell you bout a man name Willie!' My mother's fist comes down hard and sudden as a thief on his shoulder-blade. My brother runs wailing into the house and through the back door.

If Mister Papacita is in the rum part of Maas Tom's shop playing dominoes you linger on your errands, pretending it is politeness that keeps you hovering in back of the line while you wait on the bigpeople to finish their purchases. Amid

144

the slam of dominoes on formica table tops, the chink of ice in rum glasses, and the drift of cigarette smoke weaving the air and the noise and laughter into a plaited warmth, Mister Papacita sings his trademark songs:

Ah go tell yu bout a man name Willie!

The domino voices pick up the tune, warm with laughter.

Ah go tell you bout a girl name Sue!
If Ah tell you bout how dem kill i'!
What is dat to youuuuu!

'Hey, Papacita, mind youself yu know. Is how you know so much bout Willie an Sue business? You was there? Watch yuself yu know boy, watch yuself!'

The domino game erupts. 'A no dat yu fi seh! Yu fi seh Miss Aita better watch him!'

'Watch me? Cho, she cyaan watch me, man, me too slippery fi har!'

'A Ho! A Ho! So you a mongoose!'

Amidst roars of laughter the ribald chorus turns another of Mister Papacita's songs against him:

Mongoose bredda wha mek you head so red
Mongoose bredda wha mek you head so red
A mus good fire mek de wood so red
A burnin bush we a go call you
A burnin bush we a go call you!

Sooner or later Maas Tom catches us listening and sends us

145

out into the robbed, empty air. We run all the way home, proving our diligence.

Mister Papacita lived in Baltree but had his piece of ground in Maggotty on the long green slopes over the banks of the River Raiding, and all day long as he hoed among his yam hills and weeded cane, the rich music flowed with the river's singing up to the heavens as Mister Papacita heaved the hoe or the fork into the warm earth, syncopating his swing and thrust, thrust and swing, with deep sweet grunts like a one-man chain gang:

> If Ah tell you bout a man name Wille, huh huh!
> If Ah tell you bout a girl name Sue! Huh huh!

People passing shouted back in unison, caught the ball of song and threw it back to Mister Papacita over the echoing hills the way we children did, singing all the way until they had lost Mister Papacita and he had lost them behind the river's curves and the long noisy waterfall by Maas Vernon's piece of ground. But sometimes they still went singing along, the music full inside their private parts.

Mister Papacita beat the gerreh drums and led the chanting at all our wakes, tracked the Sankey at all our funerals, and sang at Baltree district's few and far between weddings. Few and far between because in our district people didn't so much go to church to get married, they mainly lived together until all the children were grown and there were no more mouths to feed, and then they went to church in Maas Levi Chevrolet and a black suit and a long white dress with a lacy train flowing down to the ground and all the grandchildren as flowers girl and page boy. Mostly only people who were in they church and don't want to live in sin married young in our district, but sometimes some other people who were young married to show they have money or that they decent too. Living together long wasn't exactly indecent but it wasn't exactly decent either. Living together short was slackness.

It was a thing to see how it was a different Mister Papacita at a wedding. You couldn't believe how this carnival giver of jokes take off the rainbow-colour rags and patches of him everyday self like how you take off drudging clothes and stand up straight and long and tall in a starch, pointy pointy collar that push up him long tall face so that it kinda look like a donkey face, likkle maaga, likkle sad. Him look sober and black and respectable, and when dem call him fi sing him stand up under the wedding booth straight and stiff like him go bury, in him one good serge suit that Maas Don the tailor mek and press smooth smooth. When him open him mouth is not the chum chukuchum chukuchum sound of gerreh drum and spirit that come out but a sound that wiggle it finger like a strong-back snake straight down yu spine and make a dive and a loop and scissors up sharp through the roof of yu skull so every single hair end on yu head stand up straight. Is like smaddy twang a instrument that is guitar and bass drum in one and the sound turn the whole of Baltree housetop them into a cathedral roof and yu feel holy. As him sing, the more him sing, Mister Papacita whole body start get excited and yu can see it a thrum and vibrate like the drumful of song inside him too big to hold in him frame, is like a riverhead coming down under the load of November rain. Him don't move and him don't twitch but yu can see as if strings stand up inside him and him left leg start beat, start beat out the well of tune inside him gainst the booth dirt floor. Like spirit take him over, jus like Effie when she warn.

147

After a while is like him whole body singing, musicking, and yu feel that all the carnival joking tek back seat and this is the real Mister Papacita, that this man born for this, born to sing organ music like church choir and holiness. Him sing song like 'Girl of my Dreams' and 'Blest Be the Ties that Bind' and yu feel there is no difference between the two, the two of them is hymn same way. And is like is not just yu head grow, the whole a yu grow and get bigger than yuself, jus hearing Mister Papacita sing at a wedding. People use to wipe them eye.

'Bwoy, that boy Papacita can sing you know, is God gift, but why that boy never go a church? Never even darken the door?' It was a strange thing for Miss Aita don't leave the Church of God church, every Sunday service, every Wednesday night Bible study and prayer meeting, every harvest and rally, and she going out on visitation and street meeting and open air crusade same way too. She try coax her husband but Papacita not taking her on, and Miss Aita telling Miss Zetta, you know, I not going beat out meself or chat chat up me mout too much on Papacita for that is not the way, that is not God way for Him don't nag none of us and even the prodigal son Him allow him and lef him fi see that time longer than rope. Next thing me go nag him and turn him off, then we have marriage problem and haffi go see parson, for yu know man don't like woman ruling over them. So I jus prayin and trustin the good Lord for Him say a good example from the wife can win the husband so is jus prayin I prayin and trustin. And she giving testifimony in church saying is a hard road for my husband not save and my heart bleed to see it and how him far from the peace of the Lord but I am pressing on brethren I am pressing on please pray for me while I pray for myself in Jesus name and the

148

church people moaning and saying ah sister, ah sister, we will pray for you in Jesus name.

Mister Papacita not going to any church and he laughing at the Church of God people who sometimes come to hold prayer meeting in the house with Miss Aita and try to catch him and preach to him before he can slip out the backdoor of the house. Sometimes, just like mongoose, he slip them, but sometimes like mongoose they catch him too, and they coulda preach to him like Paul, Mister Papacita just laugh and say, 'Awright Miss Julett, awright Miss Berbett, Ah soon come. Soon as me get me new shampatta me wi come' and you knew he was making fun for shampatta is a ole slave shoes make out of old car tyre that nobody don't wear any more, not even the Jeremiah Watkisses. Or sometimes he would say, 'Awright, Miss Berbett, soon as Maas Phillip ready, me wi come right backa him.' Maas Phillip was Miss Berbett husband that was another one famous for not going to church with his wife, and if she talk too hard him give her a touch or two with the supplejack.

Mister Papacita laughing at all the churchpeople and all his wife prayers to save him but Miss Aita is the sweet Dulcinea to him Don Quixote and nothing on God's good earth can't come between them. They have neither chick nor chile and that is why they have time to behave like they is young chicken Miss Zetta say, and Miss Nellie nod her head boy yu telling me, a true, true word. Nobody coulda understand those two for they don't behave like nobody else in the district, only maybe Minna and Cudjoe Man when they was courting in secret and Miss Nellie see them from her wide Maaga Bay window. Sometimes you pass the house you see the two of them romping in the front yard that Mister Papacita plant up nice nice with june roses and Joseph coat

149

and ginger lily and stinking toe, romping like two likkle pickni that just get let out of school and Miss Aita running rings round Mister Papacita and laughing till she haffi hold her belly like she go drop.

'Cry cree!'

'Cree, Papacita! Cree!'

And Mister Papacita grab her up and hoist her up in the air even though Miss Aita kinda big and fat, and the two of them stagger and lean gainst the house laughing to catch they breath. It was nothing for the two of them to dress up in they good clothes like they going wedding and take outing by theyself, but nobody ever know where they go except we sure is not obeah man for Miss Aita is a serious God-fearing woman eena her church and who either she or nice nice Mister Papacita have malice against fi go obeah? Even Miss Nellie kibber her mouth, though she pass remarks bout how Papacita laughy laughy too much for a big man, just like him cousin Netta Purcell that go asylum, and bout how Miss Aita behaving unseemly for a churchwoman and the church shoulda call her up, even take her one side and whisper in she ears to set better example in she yard for the young people coming up, and furthermore for that same heathen husband, and some of the people in the district agree. Anyway, Miss Aita and Mister Papacita going on they way not too paying anybody any mind and Miss Aita smiling nice and sweet to everybody she pass howdy Maas Tom, the Lord bless you Miss Nellie may his grace keep and sanctify you today, how you do Miss Aita, praising the Lord, me sister, praising the Lord, giving thanks and kibbering me mouth, and Mister Papacita playing his domino game at Maas Tom shop six o'clock every evening and giving laugh fi peas soup and singing the sweet songs that he make up out of his own head and teasing the children with when he find us on the road.

Then Miss Aita get the cancer and dead. Tek sick sudden so and just go into the hospital put under x-ray and dead. When they open her out for the autopsy they find black chalk in the whole of her chest, is so the wicked cancer like pimento fire eat out the woman sweet sweet flesh, wickeder than a yam thief in the middle of the night.

◆

In the Church of God church Miss Aita lying stiff and straight in the coffin on its stand with the four wheels, her two hands folded on her chest like a cross and her face quiet and soft, not matching the stiff taffeta and white that they dress her and burying her into. Not matching the way her body stretch out straight straight like they setting her up to slide soft and easy through the narrow gate that leadeth from death unto salvation. She look like how Mister Papacita look when him stand up stiff to sing at wedding and the music don't start flow riverhead through him body yet. The organ music playing sad and low and you can smell the church full of flowers, lilies and pale june roses, and beeswax from new honey that they use to polish up the floor, and women's new black dresses and sweetscent and Mildex and Pears soap and Johnson's baby powder, and you can hear some of the man dem new shoes a squeak on the shine shame-looking-glass floor. People coming and going hush-hush and rustling and soft, walking up to the coffin to look at Miss Aita lying in her last earthly home and walking back down to they seat to pick the bones of this predicament in hushed undersea whispers but what a way the woman look sweet ehn, just like she not

151

dead yu can really see say she was a saved woman and she gone to her eternal rest but what a thing ehn young young girl cut off in the prime of her life is so it go me dear that is why we have always to be ready yes ready for we know not the day nor the hour our life is not our own it is all in God's hands but me dear how poor Papacita go manage she was him light and him lamp and him oil, no dead him go dead now too him can't manage this? But Ah tell yu yu know Miss Zetta, is a sign to that boy yu know, is a sign that yu can't put all yu egg in human basket the flesh is dust and it will fail yu, maybe now he will turn to God, yes, yu know yu right Miss Emma, is a sign. Yes, is a sign.

After a while the parson come in in him cris black suit and mount the pulpit and all the congregation rise and you hear a sound, a deep deep sound that say follow me now, and music fall out the people mouth like a ripe fruit that burst in the sun and drop out a flood of seed, 'O Lord my God when I in awesome wonder!' but is Miss Kittie playing the organ, not Mister Papacita voice. And drum and shake-shake and tambourine rise up and join in the organ music for is so the Maaga Bay Church of God people sing. And it must be that the people paying tribute to Mister Papacita or else is because so much heathen and Pocomania and Church of God people in the church that day, for I never hear a singing like that in the Wesleyan church again. All sort of colour of the rainbow like Mister Papacita's carnival flags of songs leap out in the singing, crisscrossing the black lightning strokes of grief that thrumming in the undertone, as if the peopledem turn the cloth of they grief and stitch it over on the weft, turning the well of tears into a exaltation. But after the song done yu can hear some people sniffing, sniffing and moaning in that way that women moan, like they rocking theyself and comforting theyself with the grief. 'Hup! Hup! Hup!' Effie say, drawing big breath, and as the pastor signal to the congregation to sit down Effie begin, 'Lord have mercy, Lord have mercy, ban yu belly' as if she begging Jesus to ban Him belly, and same time sudden so Mister Papacita get up and leave the funeral and never come back. Is him brother Silbert have to stand for him at the rest of the proceedings.

And that is how the drinking begin. And the mashing up of the house and the howling. Mister Papacita howl in the same present tense that him use to sing him bright gold singing, him howl in the same bright colours him use to fling him out-of-order rhythm cross the domino game and him singerman cry like a jokify knight cross the charmed children's lives.

Mek Ah tell yu bout a man name Willie!
Mek Ah tell yu bout a gal name Sue!

But Mister Papacita can barely walk when him singing this now for him drunk as a bat, and sometimes you can see the tears leaking out the sides of his eyes shine like a snail trail down a wall in the dark.

One a dese fine fine time one a dese fine fine time!
Ah go bruk dung de house
Ah go bruk dung de house
Ah go bruk dung de house …
An g'way!

This was the sign that Mister Papacita was totally gone, the evenings when his pain was really bad and the drink drowned him.

He joked in the domino games, flashes of his old rainbow selves:

'But what a foolish woman though, ehn? Look how she jus up an lef me – you see how de foolish woman run 'way from progress?'

Or, appealing in mock disgust to the men on the shop piazza, 'You tink this woman have any right to up an lef me like that, ehn? You tink de woman have any right fi lef me? You don't tink Ah should *Gleaner* her say she still responsible fi me debts that me owe? Ehn? You tell me now.'

But when him blind drunk and mashing down the house him shouting 'Aita! Aita! You damn blasted idiot, wheh de arse yu gone?'

Miss Zetta and Miss Nellie made dire predictions and the Church of God churchpeople prayed. Maas Silbert trying to take him home plenty evening but is a hard job him take on because more time Mister Papacita knock him down and shout out, 'Lef me alone! Lef me alone! Yu tink me is blasted cripple me cyaan walk fi meself?' Usually sometimes the domino men help him but Mister Papacita strong bad, must be all dem strongback sarsaparilla and cow head Miss Aita use to give him, Mass Bollo say. And they pushing and pulling Mister Papacita into the house and Mister Papacita resisting and bawling out a lyrics he just make up for the occasion:

Waters get me funny
Waters get me funny!
But Ah trang like a lion
Ah trang like a li-onnnn!
Let me go oonu damn arse idiot!

And in the night in the darkness of the house and the early
morning rising with the sun:

> Ah go bruk dung de house
> Bruk dung de house
> Bruk dung de house
> An g'way!

And you wondering if him singing lying on the cold pitch-
pine floor or him manage to crawl up and lie down in the
bed.

Him start get ragged and not taking care of himself
and Miss Nellie say at the rate Papacita going him have more
drink in him now than Morris Hole River, and him brain
done pickle like mackerel inna brine, and is long time she
saying to herself that boy laughy laughy too much, and him
come from mad breed like Netta, and you know, sometimes
you see a thing happen and it look unexpected but plenty
time is cover up just like Jonkunnu, and you never know
what was really happening underneath, but things don't
really happen sudden so, they brew and boil up from long
time slow like river come over, clear from Gutter Head to
Morris Hole but it take a whole day to reach Morris Hole, is
just because you don't know. Is plenty thing Aita was hiding.
She say that to Miss Florrie, and Miss Florrie cut her eye and
chups and walk off into her house, for everybody well sorry
bout what happen to Mister Papacita.

But we children were lost in grief for the loss of our
friend, who either no longer played with us because he was
too drunk to notice, or played only half-heartedly, trying to
hide his half-heartedness under the lids of his eyes. But we
knew, as children always know, and because now slowly his

songs came coloured blue and green and pale yellow where before they were rose red and orange and flame. The organ, the four-string guitar, went silent under the flat bass blue, a jazz without a saxophone. And sometimes he would say, 'Tomorrow, chickadee, tomorrow, right now the instriment want tune. Haffi tek it to Cappie John blacksmith shop, then Ah come sing again for you.'

'Yes, Mister Papacita, evening Mister Papacita, next time Mister Papacita,' we said in whispers or bright voices, trying to send him through the fingers of our sound the touch of our loss and understanding. And we went home with our heads leaned down and our hearts feeling pale and sad, the way I imagined the bleeding heart of Jesus felt with the wound in it on the boarding up of my mother's front hall, after all the blood had drained out and left His edges blue.

Mister Papacita might have gone on like this indefinitely if what happened didn't happen. Him take to drinking not only after six o'clock but straight in the middle day now, right through the day, and after a while him take to preaching on the roadside, standing up on Arawak Wall corner the livelong noonday sun rocking on the balls of his heels and chanting, his speaking voice now as resonant as when he used to sing, 'Barber! Berbett! Nellie! Oonu must serve God, else oonu go dead, hear! Winne, Zetta, Chisel Bwoy, Lazzy, oonu must serve God, hear! Marshall, Cinco, Rat! Cudjoe Man! Blue! Oonu must serve God, else oonu wi dead, hear!' until the whole thing became like another song, horribly black and blue. Mostly he was just calling neighbours' names, not really noticing who was passing by, for his head was always leaned down with its load of drink. Then one day sudden so Mister Papacita just drop down right in the middle of the road, drop right down, and Maas Silbert come and take him up and carry him to hospital and they keep him for bout three week while they drain him out or dry him out – I forget which Maas Silbert say the doctor say, but I imagine the doctor turning Mister Papacita upside down like a pudding pan on a kitchen dresser so all the rum could leak out. And I wonder to myself if all the rum of months and years can leak out just like that in three weeks, and I want to ask my mother but I don't ask her.

Anyways when Mister Papacita come out the hospital he come back thin thin and quiet, he don't talk at all, he don't sing. Quiet and sudden so he stop, not like somebody pick up guitar and smash it so it make a big noise when it broke, but like somebody leave it in water and little by little, one by one when you not looking, the strings they melt out and just dissolve under the cool and silent flow. He stop the drinking too and he going to his bush more regular now, more like when Miss Aita was alive, but you get a feeling his heart not in it and when he not riding Vilma you notice he walking slow, not like a old man but more like he tired tired. Couple time the Church of God people from the church that Miss Aita used to go go and look for Mister Papacita, for they say is for Miss Aita sake for she was their church sister in Christ and she ask them with her last dying breath to pray for Papacita and take care of him so they will meet again in the Promised Land, but Mister Papacita tell them not to come back and the women go away. But we praying for you me brother we praying for you amen for we sister Aita and sweet Jesus sake. My brother Tony overhearing over the fence take him suck finger out of him mouth and start to laugh, 'prayin for you, prayin for you for sister Aita and sweet grater cake.'

'Come outa me yard', Mister Papacita tell the

churchpeople quiet quiet like Pappy Lazzy when he want to show you he dignify, not like the in-between Mister Papacita who woulda run them out with some strings of the national cloth that blue up the air when he blind drunk, or the old Mister Papacita who woulda just laugh and say, 'Awright Miss Julett, awright Miss Berbett, Ah soon come. Soon as me get me get me new shampatta me wi come', or 'Soon as Maas Phillip ready, me wi come right backa him.'

But one day Mister Papacita take up and start sudden so going to the Wesleyan church in Pan Land behind our house. Put on him black wedding suit and take up the Bible that Miss Aita give him but him never read and land himself in the church, not a word said to a soul. A lot of talking start to fly and all sort of version of how it go passing from mouth to mouth in the district, so it hard to work out what really happen. Maas Bollo who is a man not given to exaggeration and stirring up excitement say Mister Papacita was in him front room sitting on the bed facing Pan Land where he could hear and see right into the church gullet, from the red shine strip of floor like a tongue that lead up between the pews, right up to the parson like a skull at the altar, and the people was singing 'Nearer my God to Thee' and Mister Papacita get up sudden so like a string jerk under him breastbone and give out one almighty scream and run straight from the bed into the Wesleyan church and drop on him knee right at the altar. And two weeks later him give testifimony and the parson baptize him. The Wesleyan church was never so full as that day Mister Papacita baptize for the whole district go, and the whole churchyard full up to the brim, and Mister Papacita stand up in the baptism pool and when the pastor say, 'Aaron Purcell' (and is the first time we hear Mister Papacita real name as so often happen with people and they

name in our district), 'Aaron Purcell do you confess Jesus
Christ as personal Lord and Saviour?' Mister Papacita say
'yes' in a loud strong voice and then he ask permission to
give his testifimony in song and the parson say yes and Mister
Papacita stand up there in the baptism pool with the pastor
hand on him shoulder and sing 'Amazing Grace' and the
whole crowd hush even the boys outside craning against the
window and making joke and laughing at people hat and
spike heel, for Mister Papacita voice come back from the
grave and come forth like four-string guitar and saxophone
and organ and holy oil, and tears start run down some people
face for the sound rich and pure like Mister Papacita at a
wedding celebration and is like the Holy Ghost self stand up
in the church conducting, and I couldn't see Mister Papacita
feet under the water but I just imagine how that foot beating
time against the pool floor and him whole body vibrating
like riverhead under the weight of November rain. When the
song near to finish some people tongue loose and they start
to sing too and sudden so the whole congregation bust out
and the sound rise up and cathedral the whole of the church
and the overflowing churchyard and Baltree housetops from
Green Town to Maaga Bay, and bawling bruk out and Effie
start warn, 'Hallelujah Jesus! Hallelujah!' and even the boys
in the windows making holy noise too and that day plenty
plenty people go to the altar and get save but afterwards
plenty of them come out and go to the Church of God
church for they say the Wesleyan church cold, no spirit not
in there and they prefer Miss Aita church, and some come
out and don't go back to any church at all. Is dem sort there
the Bible talk bout, my mother say, going to church for the
fish and the bread, thinking noise is Holy Ghost, and you
see that shallow soil that the seed spring up in and no time it

withered and dead? For noise can't save nobody and is that they suppose to know but you see they refuse the truth and turn they back on God righted church where you learn to be holy and quiet before the Lord. Is the Adventist church my mother mean and this time I so studying Mister Papacita I don't bother to give her trouble and tell her that no matter what she say, as soon as I grown I going to the Baptist church on Breadnut Hill or the Church of God church in Maaga Bay for I prefer how the two of them sing. But the whole thing really strange to me, for the singing that baptism day never sound like no carnival that people put on and throw off and then come back the next day, it did sound like it coming down from a strange river with a different beat that moving both Mister Papacita leg and the peopledem in a way that they nor me couldna choose nor understand. Nor could I describe the colour of that singing, and my lack of words keep me chained, searching for it for ever.

But still and all some people leave.

Mister Papacita never leave, he stay at the Wesleyan church, nobody know why, not even Miss Nellie, though you don't think him shoulda want to honour him wife memory and go to the church where her heart was set, ehn, you don't think so, Miss Florrie? Well, yes is true, Miss Nellie, but you know, the heart knoweth its own sorrow, Miss Nellie, the heart knoweth its own sorrow, and maybe he really can't stand to remember. Is true. Is true.

Whether it true or not, Mister Papacita never leave the Wesleyan church, never go to the Church of God church where they sing in technicolour and use up drum and shake-shake and tambourine, he prefer the quiet soft Wesleyan church where the quiet is a deep deep blue its corners shading into the green-dark of the cry of barble doves and you get

160

loud noise there only when is funeral or celebrity baptism and the whole place full up of heathen and Pocomania and churchpeople from the two loud church in Maaga Bay and Breadnut Hill. Every Sunday morning when we going to the river for the washing because my mother is Adventist and not Sunday worshipper, we meet Mister Papacita on the road. He dress well and smiling at us with a light in him face that make us feel glad but still he change, he don't sing the old songs any more and he don't play domino in the rum side of Maas Tom shop any more, where the men knocking their rum glasses on the formica table tops and slamming down the domino with noise and laughter like life self and telling jokes in the warm and smoky plaited air.

On Sunday mornings Mister Papacita's voice coming out the church sounding rich and round and holy and shivers still go down you spine and you head still grow, but he don't sing red and orange and flame any more and I really miss the old jokey songs, 'If Ah tell yu bout a man name Willie! If Ah tell yu bout a gal name Sue!' But still and all I still glad for the black and white with the deep maroon streak running through it that his singing has become, for it give him back to us even though he's different now. For I understand now like bigpeople that is life changes, is life changes, Mister Papacita no longer a knight but a pilgrim who has rested from his labours and is journeying upward to the pearly gates. And after a while I get to love too the array of silver drums and mauve that his voice turn singing now in the evenings, sweet and strange as another life. Sometimes in the undertimbres of his voice I catch glimpses of something more hauntingly beautiful than I can imagine, like the day the people sang at the baptism, and then this new Mister Papacita draws me like a flood.

But mongoose-like, he slipped away from me through the fingers of doors I was not swift enough to catch to close or prise apart.

And a part of my heart, seduced, rebels. For surely God own the rainbow and the colours and the wide open world so why Mister Papacita can't sing red and gold and sweet orange any more? And I saying to myself that maybe is because he don't forget Miss Aita death yet and not because he start going to the wrong church like some people say and I looking up to the sky to see if I can see God, and I sending up a prayer saying God Mister Papacita is like a picture that somebody draw in the outside frame but the middle don't fill in yet, the part where you take the crayon and criss cross criss cross till the picture shining and you feel satisfy. So please God full back in Mister Papacita colours so we can hear the real Mister Papacita again.

But though in Sabbath School the teacher say we must have faith when we pray I have a feeling that when and if God fill in the blanks it won't be the same Mister Papacita that I know and love, that though it won't be the in-between Mister Papacita that use to sing pale blue and green or the other Mister Papacita that don't sing at all, it will still not be the same, he will be different still, just like how I love him different now. For how you go love a person the same when they change from red and orange and gold to maroon and black and white, and blue? When him turn a strange man, kneel down, singing in the shadow of mauve-blue silence and green-dark barbledove green?

But I kinda confuse for I still wondering bout the colour beyond colour that the people sing that baptism day. I listening to hear if Mister Papacita ever sing it full again, and maybe him sing it and maybe him don't sing it or maybe my ears seal off no matter how I listen, for all I hearing is no red and orange and only maroon white and black, and blue. But time will tell, Miss Nellie always say, and she should know, for is long time now she talking things that she don't really know about or understand.

EPILOGUE: A BEGINNING

The year I left the district was three years after the old Mister Papacita died. The morning before I was to leave for Kingston and the teachers' college I went down the mango walk to Morris Hole River and looked out to the sea. The mist was still on the water so silence could not hear my footsteps cool and enwrapped as dacron sheets, but I waited standing on the riverbank, shivering with cold until the sun came up and I could see all the way down the river's murmur and its snake, out to where cool breezes came off the sea towards Lucea town. The riverbanks and the tall trees made a funnel that narrowed in and in and the patch of blue at the far end was the intimation of the sea.

I thought about the district and I thought about everyone in it and I thought about me. Then I was very afraid but excited and glad to be leaving at the same time. Later I thought and knew that I was me and all of them, Effita and Ray and Mister Papacita and Cudjoe Man with his daughter with the Christmas tree hair, and my mother and my father with the supplejack coming into the room to threaten but not to beat, and my brother running through the room wailing Mister Papacita's songs. I thought how they were all so different with all their different secrets that I could never know and yet I knew them all like a single person masquerading names like changing selves, I knew them all because they were all the people I had been and there was no me before there was them.

The river has never failed me, even in going back. That morning I stood in the river's window and I knew that for the time it was all right, because always there would be the river and beyond it the glimpse of the sea.

Glossary

ackee	a yellow fruit with bright black seeds; grows in groups of three in a red pod
blue boot	best clothes (idiomatic). 'Wear blue boot fi go climb eleven step' is an expression meaning 'put on your best clothes to go to the courthouse'
bulla cake	round, flat cake
congotay	deceitful; deceiver; you are deceived
cotta	a circular pad made from twisted cloth, used to cushion a load borne on the head
cry cree	plead for mercy, ask for a reprieve, usually in fun, as for example in a game
cucumakka stick	a small branch of the very hard wood of the cucumakka tree, or a stick made from it. It has no abortifacient properties
dead bad at sun hot	(proverbial) 'Will come to a bad end in the middle of the day'
dulcimina	an old-fashioned suitcase
duppy	ghost
facety	rude, impertinent, forward
fahleetee	an exclamation meaning 'Good grief!', 'Oh no!' or 'I don't believe it!' *'Yu fahleetee'* or 'nuh fahleetee' means 'so much that you wouldn't believe it'
faas with	be rude to someone; or interfere with someone's personal business. When used to mean 'be rude to', the phrase means the same as 'facety with'
four eye	someone with supernatural foresight or the ability to discern hidden things. 'Have four eye' means to have such foresight or ability
Gleaner	the name of a leading daily newspaper, often used generically to mean 'newspaper'. When used as a verb 'to *Gleaner*' means 'to make an

166

	(embarrassing) announcement in the newspaper, about someone or something'
gourd	a vessel made from a joint of bamboo
grater cake	small cake made of grated coconut cooked in white sugar and decorated with red colouring
hootiah	literally, someone who lives in the bushes; a person who has not been well brought up
jacket, to give jacket	to name a man as the father of a child when he is in fact not the father
jigger	an insect that can burrow under the skin
kibbering	from 'kibber yu mout', which means to keep your mouth shut, be discreet in what you say
mirasmi	malnutrition
mouthamassy	(literally, 'mouth, have mercy!') Person who gossips or constantly raises his/her voice in quarrels
Pocomania	a religious cult merging Christian and traditional African beliefs and practices
puss back foot	(idiomatic). The phrase 'dress no puss back foot, dress like puss back foot' means to be very well dressed
puss boot	a soft-soled canvas shoe
Sankey	an old hymn book written by David Sankey, a singing evangelist and composer. 'To track the Sankey' means to read a Sankey hymn aloud line by line so the listeners can sing in tandem
so-so	barely OK, in neither good nor bad shape, neither happy nor sad
tegereg	an uncouth, war-like, trouble-making person
toofenkeh	good-for-nothing; down-and-out person
UC	University (of the West Indies) Hospital
warn with machete	give a stern warning
yaws	a persistent sore

STUDY NOTES

BY JOYCE STEWART

Heinemann

These study notes have been included to provide guidance for students and teachers studying *Songs of Silence* for the *CSEC®* examination. The notes have been developed to meet the requirements of the new syllabus, and to help students to develop a clearer understanding of the novel in terms of its context, themes and structure. The questions and activities throughout the notes can be used in class, for homework and as exam practice, and have been designed to encourage students to analyse the text and form their own conclusions from it. These notes are not intended to replace a close reading of *Songs of Silence*.

Joyce Stewart is from Barbados, and currently teaches writing at the University of the West Indies, Cave Hill. She has over 30 years of teaching experience, ranging from teaching literature in secondary schools to lecturing courses at Cave Hill, and has authored a number of study guides and English Language publications. She is currently the Chief Examiner for English A at CXC.

STUDY NOTES CONTENTS

INTRODUCTION

1 The revised CSEC English 'B' syllabus, May/June 2012 and beyond

1.1 The revised CSEC English 'B' syllabus differs slightly from previous syllabuses.

There are two papers. Paper 1 is 90 minutes long, consisting of three questions from the three basic genres: drama, poetry and prose fiction. Each question will require five to seven short answers. This paper carries 36 per cent of the total marks.

1.2 Paper 2 is two hours long, and requires essay-type answers to **three** questions, one from each genre: drama, poetry and prose. This paper carries 64 per cent of the total marks.

- In the drama section, knowledge of only one text is required. There is a choice of two questions on this text.
- In the poetry section, there is a choice of two questions. One question is based on two **named** poems in the text. The other allows candidates to use any two appropriate poems from the prescribed list in their answer.

1.3 In the prose section, there are six questions. Students may either:

- answer a question (a choice of two is offered) on either of the two prescribed novels or
- answer a question (a choice of two is offered) on the prescribed short stories.

1.4 *Songs of Silence* is one of the two prescribed novels in the prose section. Students will therefore be required, if they so choose, to study this text in detail. The syllabus emphasizes that the following elements of prose fiction must be studied, taught and understood:

(a) Narrative technique and the use of first-person and third-person narrators.

(b) Structure, that is, the way in which a work of prose fiction is put together, for example, whether it is an unbroken narrative or a narrative divided into chapters, or into larger sections, or more than one narrative put together to form a longer narrative.

(c) The difference between narration and description.

(d) The presentation of humankind in a social setting.

(e) Characterization.

(f) Themes.

2   Reading Songs of Silence

To answer a question effectively on *Songs of Silence* (or any other work of literature), you must read the novel at least three times.

2.1   **The first reading** is primarily so that you become familiar with the plot and the main characters, and get some idea of the setting of the novel. You should complete this reading without any reference to notes or criticism or commentary.

Following the first reading, you should do some background work. Find out about the time period in which the novel is set, and about the author. You can start by using the information in these notes for this, but also do your own research by looking at books in the library, or using the internet.

2.2   **The second reading** involves close reading of the text, making notes and observations as you go along. Try to focus your notes under a series of headings, e.g. characterization, key theme(s), structure, narrative technique. When you are finished you will find that you have developed considerable insight into the novel.

Following the second reading, you should then begin reading the notes and commentary provided on the novel. See how many of the observations you agree with, or have picked up on your own. Remember too that you are free to disagree with what critics or observers have said or written about the book, once you can defend your point of view **with evidence from the text.**

2.3   **The third reading** is another close reading, where you begin to assemble your various perspectives on the novel. You can feel yourself ready to present a position or defend one, on some aspect of the novel. After this reading, you should look at the section headed 'Guidelines for Examination Preparation'. Begin outlining possible answers to the questions listed, as well as to the other questions your teacher provides or you may have seen elsewhere.

3   Writing essay answers

Essay-type answers to examination questions on literature texts require that you read the question carefully. Try to determine exactly what you are being asked, e.g. 'discuss', 'compare and contrast', 'explain', 'outline'. A glossary of these words is available at the end of the CSEC May/June 2012 English 'B' syllabus. Ask your teacher to go through the words with you, and ask for further explanation and illustrations if necessary.

Answering a literature question is like preparing a legal argument. The argument is sounder and more convincing when you can cite evidence to support a point that you are making. Evidence is generally (a) an event or set of events in the text, (b) what someone says or does or (c) what someone says about someone or something else. You need to be careful, however, especially where the last of these is concerned: what someone says about someone or something else can often tell us more about the person speaking than the person or event spoken about.

Evidence should always be complementary, i.e., one piece of evidence should support the other. Evidence that contradicts other evidence, or contradicts your argument, will damage your answer.

Direct quotation is not absolutely necessary, so there is no need to learn long quotations from the text. You can paraphrase what someone says, or describe what someone does or an event that takes place. Your best option may be a mix of direct quotation and paraphrasing.

BACKGROUND TO THE NOVEL

About Curdella Forbes

Curdella Forbes was born in Jamaica, in Claremont, Hanover. She is a teacher as well as a writer. Currently a professor of Caribbean Literature at Howard University, USA, she has also taught at the University of the West Indies, Mona, and at the high school and community college level in Jamaica.

As well as *Songs of Silence*, she has written two other books of fiction: *A Permanant Freedom* (Peepal Tree Press, 2008) and a collection of stories for young teenagers entitled *Flying with Icarus and Other Stories* (Walker Books, 2002). Her stories have appeared in the journals *Bim* and *Jamaica Journal*, and in the anthology *Survivor* (Walker Books, 2002). Curdella Forbes is also the author of the non-fiction work *From Nation to Diaspora: Samuel Selvon, George Lamming and the Cultural Performance of Gender* (University of West Indies Press, 2005).

Historical and social background

Songs of Silence is set in rural Jamaica in the 1960s. This was a period of change in the country. The Rastafarian religion was growing; teachers were being recruited to work internationally; there was an upsurge in Jamaican music. Research into the social history of Jamaica in the last half of the twentieth century shows that in the late 1950s and 1960s the unemployment rate was high in Jamaica – as high as 22 per cent of the total working population in 1962 – and the society was making the transition from a British colony into an independent territory. Considerable interest was being given to education, more particularly the kind of education being offered in a country with a long colonial history of slavery and British rule. The education provided in schools at that time had little to do with the Caribbean. The history taught, the books read and studied, the senior and administrative staff and even the school rules came from Britain. *Songs of Silence* is set in a rural area which, from the stories, had not yet caught on to the shift in behaviours that would lead to the end of colonial rule.

In a 1987 work called *Black Consciousness and Popular Music in Jamaica in the 1960s and 70s* (www.kitlv-journals.nl), Erna Brodber, a Jamaican writer, notes a number of elements that marked the social climate in Jamaica. These have some relevance for *Songs of Silence*. One of the elements is that while it was normal for the black middle class to try to claim its European connections, or at least, try to show that it 'possessed' European culture (classical music, British-style education, social behaviours), the lower class was less concerned with striving for such things. This 'lower class' was the majority. A second feature is that the ruling elite demanded literary skills and certification from those who wanted to move up the social ladder, but the plantation system worked to keep them on the land. Brodber says that 'Literate Afro-Jamaicans … tended to see this book learning not as a tool for making a livelihood, but as the ultimate truth.'

Brodber's work points out that by the 1960s, middle-class attitudes were challenged to embrace the 'Afro-centricity which long existed in Jamaica'. The change in perspective was promoted by agencies such as the University of the West Indies where there were university-sponsored talks on 'identity'.

About the stories

Songs of Silence is a novel composed of smaller stories about childhood, about certain aspects of life in rural Jamaica, about the character of the people and the things that create bonds between the people, and between the narrator and her childhood environment. It is not a novel about a central character who develops and changes, though we are able to recognize milestones in the narrator's growth through her progress in school and other comments she makes about going away. Nor is it a novel of an event and its consequences. It works more as a cultural record, telling of the nature and experiences of the community; of how it *is*, rather than how it was.

THEMES AND VALUES

A theme, in literature, is an idea or concept which an author is either trying to explore or wants the reader to think about. Writers rarely state explicitly what these themes are; they must be teased out, by looking at how the characterization and events are presented and structured. Themes rarely emerge as simple and easily identifiable; they often overlap, or have nuances which may not be evident on a first reading or casual reading.

We will consider the following themes that emerge in *Songs of Silence:*

- (a) Family
- (b) The place of the elderly
- (c) Genealogy
- (d) Education

Other themes are then suggested for further self-study.

Family

Family, real or adopted, is important in the novel. Below is a suggested list of the aspects of family you should think about when reading *Songs of Silence.*

- (a) Kinds of family structure (single parent, nuclear, extended, childless)
  - Nuclear family – Marlene's family with her parents and siblings
  - Cudjoe's family – a single-parent family, headed by a male
  - Miss Minnie and Raymond – This would at first be described as nuclear, with some peculiar features. It becomes a truly single-parent family when Raymond is 15 and his father dies
  - Mr and Mrs Papacita – Mr and Mrs Papacita have no children, but they still represent a kind of family
  - Effita's family – Effita is a senior member in an extended family.

(b) Family loyalty
- Sibling rivalry and companionship
- Parental relationships (interaction between Marlene's parents)
- Parent–child relationships (Marlene and her father; Cudjoe Man and his daughter; Miss Minnie and Raymond; Raymond and his father; the Watkiss family)

The place of the elderly

This is not a developed aspect of the novel. In fact, it is recognized only in the opening story, 'Effita'. The first story introduces the midwife as one aspect of the role and place of the elderly. A second story where it can be studied is 'Morris Hole', where the attitude to the aged is different, for various reasons. Exploring this theme can help in recognizing the origins or causes of respect for the elderly – either related strictly to race, class and the legacy of plantation life and slavery, or to dependency on one's own people.

Aunt Sare presents an unusual case: she is family, a 'grandmother', to most of the village. She can no longer be active, but has the welfare of the community at heart, and is looked after by the community in the way a grandmother is looked after by immediate family members in the home.

Task

Study the case of Marlene's father and his ancestors, the difference in the attitudes held by him and his wife. Compare Marlene's recollections of each situation.

Genealogy

An important part of 'family' in the novel is genealogy. It is particularly dealt with in the story 'Morris Hole'. It is also alluded to in the story 'Travellers, or Fathers, or Little Fool-Fool'. Genealogy is important in the Caribbean for perhaps the same reason as elsewhere – it gives one a name, and sometimes that name is seen as being helpful to one's progress in life. Slavery was not an institution we, as descendants of enslaved people, are proud to have experienced. Neither are the descendants of the slave masters: they are not proud to be associated with people who could have set up and used the practice. However, the legacies are facts of life. Across the region Europeans produced children with enslaved women, giving rise to a range of 'colour' and to degrees of status as a result of that range of colour. This is a fact of life acknowledged in *Songs of Silence*. Sometimes being able to claim kinship with those of lighter skin colour was seen as an advantage. Forbes characterizes Marlene's mother as a black woman who saw no purpose in claiming to be part of a family who did not want you to be part of them. In this she was reflecting the change of outlook developing in the region early in the 1960s. It was a movement towards Black Consciousness, an acceptance of what that meant, and a developing pride in being black.

Related aspects to consider are:
- The place of race in society (see the stories 'Morris Hole', 'Travellers or Fathers … '
- Class and social stratification.

Education

Education is valued highly in Marlene's family, and her family represents a change in outlook taking place in rural areas which once focused on the land. In the community generally, not all families place the same importance on school. Where school is mentioned in each story it is noticed that the males spend

181

comparatively little time in school, particularly at times of planting and reaping, and almost never on Fridays. Well-to-do families send their sons every day, and most girls are allowed to go to school all week. Apart from Ezekiel Watkiss, who does well in school and in later life as a contractor, the boys seem headed for land and farming, which gives them security. The wave of change which is starting in the rural areas has not yet reached the village.

Other educational themes to consider might include:
- The education of boys in rural areas
- The education of girls
- The value of educational outcomes: refer to Marlene; Ezekiel; Raymond; Raymond's half-brothers.

Other aspects to explore:

- Male–female relationships:
    - Cudjoe Man and Minna; Mr and Mrs Papacita; Marlene and Ezekiel
    - Marlene and Raymond; Marlene and Ezekiel Watkiss
    - Marlene's parents
- Superstition and folklore:
    - The noname woman and her pregnancy
    - Special (supernatural) gifts: Marlene, Nathan, the noname lady
- Change:
    - Stories best indicating change include 'The Idiot,'' 'Miss Minnie', 'Morris Hole', 'Travellers, Fathers … ' and 'So Few and Such Morning Songs'.
    Changes include growing up; the development of relationships; migration. Changes in the lives of the younger generation lead to a broadening of experience, while the older generation, despite the acquisition of means to change, seems to settle in more securely. Consider that Raymond provides

Miss Minnie with the means of changing her life style but she cements herself into the village and her old attitude of service. Mr Papacita has change thrust on him, but though he changes superficially, he too remains firmly entrenched in the village.

Task

Study the stories listed, and note the specific changes that are recorded. How is Marlene affected by these changes? How is the community affected?

NARRATIVE TECHNIQUE AND STRUCTURE

Narrative technique

Narrative voice

Marlene, the girl 'narrator', is the central consciousness and voice of all the events and stories. Her narration is a weave of various strands. The main strand belongs to the grown-up girl narrator, but she has various selves: the very young and innocent primary school girl; the pre-adolescent and adolescent of high school; the young woman standing apart from her village and reflecting. There are also other voices which Marlene allows to take over for short intervals in the storytelling, so that we hear her mother and other adult women in the village.

Marlene's narrative voice has various tones or levels. The first of these which we meet in 'Effita' uses Standard English, and suggests the grown-up recalling and reflecting on various incidents. For instance, the first chapter starts with a grown-up voice, removed from the scene, saying:

> 'Miss Effie must have been the second oldest person in our district when I was nine.' (page 1)

When she describes the oldest person she says:

> 'Visiting Auntie Sare was both a treat and a fearful experience.' (page 1)

The second tone comes as the writer lets the consciousness of the little village girl strengthen into telling the story and nudges the other voice away a little. Both the tone and structure change so that the little-girl aspect of the narrator captures the mood of excitement when she says:

> ' ... when Miss VeenAnn come out on the road and

grab Miss Effie in her collarbone and call her quiet
and firm by her right name ... ' (page 10)

At other times, the narrator slides into the place and voice of some
other adult villager. The exchange can be missed. For instance, in
telling the story of the noname lady the narrator begins: 'There
were stories', then slips directly into:

'she make a fool of herself over some man ... and
when attaclaps come ... he disappear'. (page 17)

Generally then, beneath the main adult voice which
introduces, describes and comments on the various situations,
there are other adult voices filling in details, along with the
consciousness of the child or young girl supplying what is the
child's perception and experience (and these may be real or
fantasy). The narrator's own description of her thought processes
is enlightening when she says:

'My head don't work straight like other people
head. Sometimes my head weave stories inside itself,
spinning a whole Anancy web of things that don't
really go so but always feel realer than the things that
go so. My Aunt Edna say is because my eye cast ...
she say cast eye is a kinda mix up four eye, your brain
don't come too straight.' (page 100)

Initially the child voice/consciousness is limited by her
mother's influence and what she overhears from other adults,
rather than her own independent understanding in relating the
details of various events and experiences. On another level the
child narrator's voice slides deep into the character and tone of
one of the villagers, with all the exciting, dramatic and descriptive
air of the village storyteller. The girl uses the folklore easily, and
sometimes there are brief and rapid exchanges of voices between
the child (suggested in the naive statements or questions) and
an adult villager. For instance, in 'A Story with No Name' there

185

are fanciful creations about the woman, using the folklore. The girl says:

> 'I was puzzled. Women only got that sort of thing when their husband die and somebody forget to plant the duppy or she forget to sleep in red panty so he can't come in the house. So the noname lady did married to the man that take her tongue then?'
> (page 24)

Her voice is replaced or answered immediately by an adult's:

> 'See it there, is bad growth she have in her stomach. Cancer, her inside blue. Woman don't use up her inside, what you expect?' (page 24)

The voice then shifts back to the child's consciousness:

> 'One night a whole heap o' whispering and footfalling and bottle lamp flickering like giant peenie-wallie on the road below the hill by Miss Vie house and somebody send to call Miss Pertiss, the Magotty and Mount Peace midwife from all the way in Retrieve.'
> (page 25)

A number of stories reflect simplicity, told as the child has the inclination and ability to interpret and tell them. The stories of Miss Effie, Cudjoe, Long Man and Mr Papacita are among those carrying that innocence for the most part. As she grows the child narrator's voice gathers more authority, particularly where the incidents described take place away from adult scrutiny, as happens in the stories about school experiences, such as 'The Idiot'.

Language

Separating narrative voice from style and language is difficult. If the narrator is going to be authentic, it is essential that he/ she uses a style and language appropriate to the society being depicted. Simply put, style refers to *how* speakers or writers say whatever they want to say: their choice of words, type(s) of sentences, kinds of figurative language.

Marlene is designed to represent the true Jamaican, growing up in the village and growing into an awareness of another way of life and expression, while being comfortable with both it and her origins. She therefore slides freely between Standard and degrees of non-Standard English as the occasion or situation demands, depending on which consciousness is uppermost at the point in the narration. When she is in 'village character' mode it is as if she has no control of the local dialect sneaking in and taking over her speech. A good example of this occurs in the story 'Miss Minnie'. Marlene starts out in Standard English:

> 'Years after when Raymond told me the story, he said the thing he could not understand was the way Miss Minnie change' (page 80)

Note that it is only the tense at the end of the sentence that takes the sentence out of Standard English as the dialect sneaks in. This continues and intensifies as Marlene goes into the story, telling it as a villager would:

> 'He don't know if he imagining it but is like she shadowing him … ' (page 81)

> 'He get a promotion and the company lend him money … He so frighten for Miss Minnie never talk like that … .' (page 81)

Her speech is made more authentic through the use of local proverbs and pithy sayings, such as the one which sums up her experience and feelings in the same story: ' ... but who feels it knows it, every tub siddung on its own bottom'. (page 87)

Style

A strategy used in the unfolding narrative is to give the audience a role to play in telling the stories – interpretation. This is based on the principle that it is important, particularly if we want to gather more from what we hear and read, to think of the meanings of words: most words have more than one meaning – meanings which are often made clear when we consider the context. To really 'read' well (recognize, understand, interpret, apply) we need to study words. When we consider the novel's title: *Songs of Silence*, our attention is taken perhaps, first with the idea of 'silence', and then about there being 'songs' – songs of silence. Is this a contradiction? How many ways do we understand the words 'song' and 'silence'? Professor Mervyn Morris has described the novel as 'inhabiting an elusive space between what is said and what is felt, what is conveyed and what is perceived ... .' What he draws our attention to is the author's use of suggestion, of the reader's interpretation, understanding and perception, rather than clear statements from the narrator, as a major part of the narrative technique. The author creates silences which we fill as we connect and make deductions from the experiences described.

Take the word 'song' which is used in the title. 'Song' is usually accepted as an arrangement of words in a lyrical or poetic form, often set to music. The kind of music helps us to interpret the words in different ways, e.g. as romantic, teasing, praising or contemplative. A 'song' is often a story, containing some history or record of persons or events. How we react to the contents is determined by the tone we perceive in the song or story-telling, and even the context of the story. One value of songs/stories is that they are ways of recording cultural history, with or without comment.

The other aspect of the title, and which itself contributes

much to the narrative technique, is the word 'silence'. Many informative discussions on 'silence' are available, easily accessible on the internet if you have the opportunity. One very informative article can be found here: www.chinamediaresearch. net/vol4no2/9.pdf.

Silence is a tool. It can be used as a stimulant: in the middle of it our minds take over, and ideas and information are stimulated. The narrator uses this reflective and stimulating kind of silence to awaken and broaden her own knowledge and her thoughts, to make connections between events. For instance, much of what she says in 'A Story with No Name' comes as a result of thinking about what is not said by the adults, by what her own thinking and imagination supply. The answers she finds to things demonstrate the value of such contemplation. Consider, for instance, when she leaves Nathan to go off on her own (page 29) and her ensuing narration about the family friend, Long Man, who would turn up unannounced, stay for a while during which time he brightened her mother's life (pages 106–11).

Silence can also be used as a tool for control or silencing. Look at the song of the noname lady: she is powerful because she fascinates the community and evokes much speculation. The more we know of a thing or person, the greater our control over it. The noname lady is perhaps the only one who knows the truth of her story and of her family, but she denies the villagers any power over her by not satisfying their curiosity and need for control. Consider why the narrator's mother silences the villager who makes insinuations about her husband (page 28).

Counsellors, pastors, sales persons and others are educated in the skill of gathering useful information which can then be used for or against the source. Such people have been trained in the art of keeping silent or of saying just enough to prompt thoughts and interventions from others. Since in most cultures people are uncomfortable with silence or empty spaces, the principle is to maintain one's own silence long enough to make the other want to fill the gap. Often the other party will seek to fill the gap, and in doing this they provide information, expose their concerns, prejudices, weaknesses or desires. 'Morris

Hole' provides the author/narrator with the kind of opportunity described above. As the narrator says 'Anything you want to think you think ... .' (page 102)

Silence also sends messages. The expression 'speaking silence' is useful for thinking about communicating ideas. In the story 'Travellers, or Fathers ...' the narrative voice never judges or actively compares Long Man and Cudjoe Man. The audience makes the comparison instead. We notice that there is relatively little on Long Man when compared to Cudjoe. Why is it that Marlene's father is never disturbed by this man's presence in his home? The silences created in the work will not be the same for all audiences, but the stories are all part of the narrator's experience: real, dreamt or imagined, and it is her single complex consciousness that unifies them into one novel.

Structure

The fictional writer usually has a view or purpose behind the chosen sequence of events, and the reader is usually able to see how one thing leads to the next. In real life we know that an action has an effect and so there is order, yet often we wonder why things happen when and how they do. Certainly, in the things we do there is usually a plan that we might share with others, but really, there are areas of life we cannot control, and natural life often appears to be random.

The stories in *Songs of Silence* do not, on the surface, appear to have a definite plan to their sequence, but since the narrator returns to her childhood and apparently recounts and reflects on incidents, places and people as the mind wills, the movement between episodes is fitting – it is true to the 'pattern' in which children think. The narrative structure in the novel then, reflects the random consciousness of a child where the moment in reality and in the imagination is what leads the story. The narrative structure in the novel then, reflects the random consciousness of a child where whatever is going on in the child's mind at a particular time is the child's focus or reality. The child's own feelings, needs and imagination lead the story and the connections between stories.

The stories are independent and could be rearranged without any meaning being lost or changed. For instance, the story 'Nathan' consciously spans the narrator's life, brings recollections of very young activities and confesses to adult mistakes and longings. As such it could have been an introductory story. Instead, the seemingly random placement of stories with their events and learning experiences reflect the unpredictable thought pattern of the child narrator. The content, not the sequence, of stories is therefore the focus. Each story is complete in itself. The novel then fits together like an album of music or songs – designed to reflect various moods and experiences, not to chart a life. Each song is finished by itself, but the mood or the event being celebrated or some theme holds the songs together.

Each story is made interesting by the use of details which enable the reader, having also experienced childhood, to identify with the aspects being described. Michael Anderson, a successful American singer and song -writer, talks about songs that tell stories and how the success of the song depends on the ability of the writer to make the audience listen, not simply hear. (See the on-line article called 'The Song Story' (www. Taxi.com/music-business-faq/songwriting/lyrics/thesongstory. php).) His comments are included here because of the title of this novel and partly because of the content and structure of *Songs of Silence*. Every new story/chapter is a 'song'. In studying the novel we should have some curiosity as to how the various chapters fit in with the idea of 'song'. Anderson gives this explanation:

> 'I am defining a ... song as one that contains the easily recognised elements of ... narrative ... beginning, middle, and end, with a recognisable story arc that contains the classic elements of drama and delivery. Like a mini short story.'

Such a description can be applied to each 'chapter' of *Songs of Silence*.

Another aspect to which Anderson draws attention is that the story-song develops like a film, moving from place to place and activity to activity, possibly

> ' ... building through anger, outrage, revenge, climax, and eventual understanding, with the character who is central to that story changing in a redemptive way.'

A good example of this occurs in the story of Minna, Cudjoe, and Samson in 'Travellers, or Fathers, or Little Fool-Fool'. The narrator carefully constructs a context for the events to be told. We are encouraged to like and respect Cudjoe Man, to like and to feel sympathy for the retarded child, like and smile at Minna, even compare Marlene's father and Cudjoe Man. Because of the scene-setting we are more inclined to respect some characters, empathize with others, share the biases suggested in the story. We participate in the drama, and generally benefit from it, and appreciate the opportunities for redemption among the characters. In fact, this story works well to illustrate the way a film involves the audience and moves in various directions in showing the various areas of setting. In the end we have our 'album', going through different feelings and moods, but tied together by one developing consciousness.

Many novels are published which attempt to weave into the main character's life information on the culture of a place. Many of them read like documentaries stressing perhaps too much, or the wrong kind of detail, or they comment on things which the narrator could not have known. Often the emotional aspect – that is the reaction to the thing or what sparked the thought in the first place is not captured and relayed to the audience: the character and situations do not feel authentic. According to Anderson, the song-writer'schallenge concerning the creative work and how it can manage to appeal to and hold the audience is summed up in the following question:

> 'Is it a fresh and interesting approach or is it predictable and similar to the way other writers

have handled the ... subject matter and emotional content before?'

You might want to compare this novel with some other works which seem to have the goal of reflecting a society but still appeal very strongly to the imagination. Anderson offers some explanation concerning why novels like *Songs of Silence* are fascinating. According to him, the inexperienced song/story-writer tends to generalize the subject and therefore the content does not hold the listener's interest. This is a weakness since the audience needs to relate to the story in the song in some way, so that they can become involved; they need details. The story/song-writer therefore needs to include what is necessary for the listener to know, the details that help the audience to be part of the real experience, so that the story moves forward in a dramatic way. The writer must be able to leave out what does not advance in the story or what clutters the story. This is why the story 'Nathan' is funny, yet serious and absorbing. Paragraph one is dramatic; it grips the attention with a tight but colourful retelling of an act.

Forbes avoids the pitfall of shutting out audience response by using the details that help us picture and react to events, but these details are conveyed in peculiar ways. As an example one can look at 'A Story with No Name'. Near the start of the story the narrator sees her father give his string of fish – his lunch, really – to a woman who is shrouded in mystery. That mystery makes the woman a large and important part of the people's lives as they are always seeking to satisfy their need for information by fabricating it themselves. The child-voice gives several details, real or imagined about the woman's life. She makes references to the narrator's father, or a man who looks like him and appears to have been connected to the woman.

There is enough space and information for the alert reader to notice things and to make connections (become involved). While the child narrator gives 'information', she is not herself mature enough to perceive any connection. For instance, the noname lady later has a baby boy whom she calls Paul. The narrator naïvely tells about a 'whisper going round for some

193

time', suggesting a connection between her father and the woman: that the little boy was her father's child. The narrator's innocent comment is:

> 'I knew what Luce said wasn't true, because I had seen my father talk to the noname lady only once, that time he gave her the string of fish.' (page 28)

A dramatic element is introduced when she gives us a snapshot of her mother 'warning Luce Blagrove with a machete' because Luce dared to repeat the rumour. Very significantly when the story ends with the little boy being eight years old to the narrator's sixteen, he still cannot speak, so the silence creating the wondering remains unbroken.

The content of the stories keeps the reader emotionally involved. Involvement is a way to hold attention. To return to the story 'Nathan', for instance, we come to expect determined, if inexplicable, action from a boy who made hard bargains before he could read or write. In the incident which resulted in his loss of a leg, Forbes captures the pompous self-praising behaviours of those who have achieved unexpected position and are insecure about people's respect. We judge and condemn the politician as soon as he asks 'You know who me is?'" (page 37) and even more so when he abuses Nathan. The audience is unable to sympathize with such a man against the fair but inscrutable Ethan. Later the narrator makes a comparison between the peace and satisfaction the grown-up Ethan has in his rural farming life, and her own adult life in the city where she is uncomfortably matched with people who cannot see or appreciate the need for silence. She describes him as having an emotional satisfaction which she needs, and gets when she visits her brother, so she keeps visiting. It is these refreshing silences which let her commune with nature and herself that keep her visiting her brother. Without describing the differences, Forbes invites the audience to value the rural place.

CHARACTERIZATION

The Narrator – Marlene

The major character in the novel is Marlene. She is shown as a small child whose innocence sees no negatives in anything concerning her parents. She typifies little girls who idolise their fathers, shown especially in 'A Story with No Name' and 'Travellers, or Fathers … '. She hero-worships brothers, particularly in 'Nathan'. As a child she is naturally focused on herself, so that she only mentions the names of siblings in passing. What she gives us is a glimpse of a large family which, in her mother's opinion, gives them enough playmates. She indicates that though they enjoyed many things together, like escaping to listen to 'bigpeople's' conversations, skating down the gully, bathing in the cold river, and singing with Mr Papacita, she knew she was different (see the story of Nathan) and had to make an effort to maintain her individual rights and personality in that large family. She recognized her special place in the way her mother spoke up for her when her bigger sister would bully, in the bond between her and her father, and in her own success at surprising and successfully pummelling her older brothers whose developing 'manness' she did not understand and resented.

The young Marlene is given to fantasizing. Of her own admission when the adult Marlene looks back at herself, she enjoyed time alone to play with ants or just to create ideas and pictures in her own mind. Sometimes she weaves the fantasy into the reality, so they are indistinguishable. Two examples of this are in her story of Long Man and of the noname lady.

Even as she enters puberty Marlene still retains her naïvety, so much so that she is puzzled and hurt when Miss Retinella and Munchie insinuate to her mother that her developing body means that she is sexually involved. Her mother defends her, but compounds the hurt in forbidding her to enjoy the pleasure of plunging in naked and romping with the others at Morris Hole.

Marlene is forced to accept some of the restrictions that come with growing up.

The grown Marlene is able to separate fantasy from reality. This is demonstrated in her reliving of the period of life when Ezekiel Watkiss had some influence on her, when she struggled to accommodate her need to achieve and her need to recognize, respect and accept the worth of others. She is forced to see herself as being a snob, and so missing out on a potentially rewarding relationship. The insightful woman in Marlene is shown in the story of Miss Minnie. The suggestion is that she is in love with Raymond when she says:

> 'I not taking on this emptiness, this space that hollow
> waiting for where a man ought to be.' (page 87)

She recognizes that being a woman brings its own pains and challenges, as she understands there is no future for her with Raymond since he needs to tell her the story of his growing up and Miss Minnie, but having told, he cannot forgive her for having heard. She is also perceptive enough to understand the confining nature of the seemingly tender and caring relationship Raymond has with his stepmother.

Marlene gives us enough to let us know she enjoyed growing up in the village, but also to let us know that its limits were not for her. She tells of her success at secondary school, of her dreams at Morris Hole of going away as she gazes into the distant horizon where river enters bay, and of her certainty of leaving when she visualized herself and Raymond standing on separate riverbanks, she alone, he flanked by Miss Minnie and his father. She confirms that she left in 'Nathan' when she speaks of her occasional visits and the need to make them so she can recharge, and in her recollections concerning Ezekiel Watkiss, when she compares her struggles to his success.

Other characters

Apart from Marlene, the characters in the stories are generally symbolic. There is therefore no rounded individual presented through a series of events that shape character in any of the stories. True to the form of the short story, each one does what is necessary to help us appreciate the experiences being explored, and each one works really to construct the character of the society in which the narrator grows. At the same time we are able to recognize how someone can emerge as being 'different' in such a rural community.

Cudjoe Man, the narrator's father, Long Man, and Raymond's father, known only as 'the father' are all structured to illustrate a variety of approaches to fatherhood or responsibility for others, and through them we are able to judge what the narrator valued among the father-figures in the village. Long Man can be taken to represent what a father was not. Clearly he cared only for himself. He evoked no warmth or deep reality from the narrator. In fact she noted that he had no real substance: 'he cast a shadow ... hologrammatically', he left no mark on anything he sat on, he came unannounced, he never offered to help in household tasks, he left without fanfare, and it was only noted in passing that he no longer came. He is valued, not for himself, but because he brought some short spark into the mother's life, so that Marlene says ' ... when he was there, all day my mother sang.'(page 107)

Of a little more importance is Raymond's father who 'liked the sound of his own self surrounding him' (page 58). Though he provided for his son, he established no communication except for the 'gruff undertone' with which he gave an instruction. At least he found a woman who lavished all her attention on the boy. His influence remained even after he died when Raymond was fifteen. The boy volunteered to leave school but Miss Minnie reminded him of what his father wanted:

' ... go to school and finish you education and get a

197

good job ... one day get to leave and go somewhere
... ' (page 60)

Unlike Long Man, Cudjoe Man settled into the community
and made an impact. Cudjoe Man has solidity, and demonstrated
strong caring for his daughter. He set up a home for her and
despite his own need for companionship, he chose to keep any
other female out of his home in order that his child would not
be disadvantaged. People in the village respected him as a man
and as a father, and he demonstrated his commitment in the way
he dressed, entertained and instructed his mentally retarded
daughter, letting her know as best he could that she was valued.

The real 'father' in the novel is Marlene's, referred to only
(and possessively) as 'my father'. Though Marlene never names
her father, she never speaks of him other than with pleasure.
He was the man who came into their bedroom waving a strap,
but not to hit anyone, just to get them quiet. He was the man
who travelled far away to seek work so as to support the family.
While he was away his presence remained in the family and
with Marlene, 'alive by the skeins of stories [she] wove in her
head' (page 138). He left them to the security of home while he
travelled, but unlike some who passed through, and contrary to
the folk-tales, he always came back. Marlene could sit outside and
stare into the gathering evenings, knowing that sooner or later
her would return, and hoist her on to his shoulder. She recounts
a story of how he carried her the long way to the clinic for an
injection, and carried her home again, except that she made him
walk extra to recover her hat (page 138) and his only concern
was that she was so sick. The dream she has of him having gone
over the sea illustrates how strong her faith in him was and that
he never let her down. He was a man 'who left his dent on things
he sat on and touched' (page 140).

Miss Minnie

Miss Minnie was not of the village. Raymond's father had travelled to a distant community to find a woman who did not know about Raymond's mother, and who was as unlike her as possible. Minnie symbolizes the dangerous effects of the wrong kind of, or too much, silence. In her willingness to let silence shape her life and hide her, at first she represents a condition under which Raymond's father wanted to live – that is, entirely in his own world, having the benefits of family and companionship, without giving them anything of himself in return. The kind of silence he created and which she later accepted became a condition which threatened the quality of life for her and Raymond.

Miss Minnie maintained the 'apartness' that allowed the silence and her only relationship was with Raymond and the things that created his welfare. Unlike Raymond's mother who had left because she could not bear the silence in their relationship, Miss Minnie herself kept silent, finding other means of cementing a relationship with the boy. She compensated by demonstrating her willingness and ability to care for the family, to endure hardship, to be resourceful and to work hard. Most importantly, she stayed with Raymond, staying in the background and supporting him while he grew up and found his place at work in Kingston.

Miss Minnie can be perhaps be seen as being possessive of Raymond, as noted when he told Marlene how Minnie had changed after his mother came back into his life. He felt as though she stalked him. Miss Minnie's possessiveness created some problems, to the point where she seemed to have lost her selfhood and sense of independence, but she had stimulated such loyalty in Raymond that he never discussed her, not even with the brothers he discovered he had.

The deterioration in Miss Minnie's behaviour, her change in character, invites the reader to see the dangers in some forms of silence: her fears and other emotions were bottled up and almost drove her mad. Raymond was faced with an angry, irrational, resentful stranger whose "face contort up like is somebody else behind the skin and she start froth and scream … she rant and rave and say how ... after she Minnie done kill out her soulcase ... she is nobody ... ." Miss Minnie seemed to recover, but another personality element surfaced, when she "sudden turn young girl and want him to take her everywhere." This phase included a clingy, stifling behaviour in which she always seemed to be hoping to catch Raymond at something. Again silence created problems, because there were things Raymond realized could have been said to bring some relief, but the long-ingrained uncommunicativeness stood in the way. There comes a point where Miss Minnie seems to be manipulating Raymond through creating feelings of guilt. Eventually Miss Minnie was diagnosed with extreme depression, brought on partly by her isolation in town away from the freedom of the country, and partly because of the years of silence. Return to the country and the assurance of Raymond's devotion restored her health to some extent, but she seemed to have developed some control over Raymond, which the narrator suspects is not healthy. Miss Minnie was comfortably settled in a modern house back in the village, but on the outskirts, and did not really form strong relationships with anyone in the village.

Effita

Effita is one aspect of the oral tradition in the rural setting, where there is limited outside contact. Her behaviour calls to mind the tradition of the classical theatre and the Chorus and the professional mourners. As she travels from village to village she seeks to condition the audience into reacting to death, while also performing an information service. Effita is a character who signals change on a basic level. Her chosen role gives her a purpose and brings her attention and recognition. Effita seems dedicated to the job she has chosen, but she in fact depicts the way death announcements were made. Since death is seldom regarded as good news she earns tolerance. On the other hand, Aunt Sare whose role has been that of delivering new life, is treated almost with reverence. She is neither likeable nor unlikeable – she simply is who she is, understood and accepted or tolerated by the 'family' community.

Nathan

From the start when we are introduced to Nathan we are impressed by that first silent, purposeful and swift action of poking his brother in the eye when such behaviour was unexpected, and we are amused at the story. It works as an introduction to a very interesting character and set of situations. The narrator's stories help us to see Nathan as being only a physically small person, both in boyhood and adulthood. We recognize him as one who uses action but very few words; who is very decisive and who has significant self-confidence. His quiet, purposeful nature is shown early in his boyhood in the story of revenge for the loss of his kite. His determination is made clear in his bargaining with his siblings. His simple and down-to-earth approach to life is clear in the story of his experience as a security guard, his apparent disregard for the thousands of dollars which he was awarded by the court, his love for his wife and for the land. Nathan is described as being deeply satisfied with his small farm, his children, his earthy wife, and the opportunities to be silent and quiet. What he had, made the adult narrator reflect on what she had lost in moving away from the village. As such he represents the enduring and necessary nature of rural Jamaica.

Long Man

Long Man is an itinerant worker, but not the typical example of one. In the narrator's consciousness he seemed to be more of an idea than a real person – 'a man of shadows and unfocused edges'(page 110). Around him he wore an atmosphere of mystery and adventure. She says that despite his size he never made a dent in anything he sat on, and when he studied the sky and forecast the weather, he appeared as a shadow. In fact, she

201

was never able to get a whole picture of him as being himself. He was an easygoing person whose presence seemed to lighten her mother's outlook, because he inspired her to sing. According to the mother, Long Man had no desire for possessions, therefore he worked to earn enough money to buy food and tobacco for a time. 'He worked only to fulfil his immediate needs' (page 110). Long Man therefore can be seen as symbolic of what the future is likely to be where there is no commitment or purpose.

Ezekiel Watkiss

The adult Ezekiel Watkiss is the opposite of Long Man. Ezekiel's character shows how education can be wrested from a situation which values it only for some. In Ezekiel the sense of being somebody was never crushed by harsh taunts or poverty. He demonstrated effort and a sense of purpose which eventually makes him the envy of educated minds like Marlene. When she, despite her thorough European-style education, is still struggling to find a place, Ezekiel has put his practical skills and patience to work to build a lucrative business.

The noname lady

As Erna Brodber points out in the article alluded to earlier (see page 177), those who considered themselves middle-class (because they owned land or were of lighter complexion) had a European orientation towards life. Their need was to foster the idea of their superiority. This lady represents the vestiges of that aspect of life in rural Jamaica where the plantation system still exerted strong influence. Such persons surround themselves with mystery to promote the class system, but in reality they can maintain the façade only with the help of the underclass, negro population.

CHAPTER SUMMARIES WITH QUESTIONS

'Effita'

The story 'Effita' introduces us to the two people who helped to form the foundation of the village: Aunt Sare who is the oldest person in the village and who 'bring most of the old people in the district into the world', and Effita, the second-oldest person in the village, who ushers them out of the world. While the house-bound Aunt Sare knows each person by sound and smell and grasps every chance to make lengthy prayers for her 'children', Effita seems to go into a trance when she is town-crying, becoming unaware of comments, and never tiring until she has spread the news and her own automatic mourning far and wide. She one day makes a mistake when she announces that a young man has died. This was after he had been shot by the constable, and taken to hospital. For Effita, the two things – shooting and hospital – meant he was dead. She lost her confidence after she had mistakenly reported his death and was embarrassed by some people, the man's mother in particular. Miss Effie, as the children respectfully called her, was totally embarrassed after the man's mother managed to get her to stop the announcing, and told her not to invite death on the young man. The villagers laughed about it for days. Later, when Miss Effie's nephew died, the truth of the various cries she used to make as she did her announcing, now had real meaning for her, so that she did not announce the boy's death. It was only at the burial that she was overcome with grief and went into a frenzy of crying and shouting, and jumped into the grave.

Miss Effie's story introduces us to two younger men in the community. These are Chisel Bwoy, the constable, and Selwyn, an ex-convict. Through them we are able to see some of the 'modern' influences on the people. The constable, imitating what he had seen law officers do in the movies called 'westerns', which depict frontier life in the early USA, shot Selwyn. Selwyn is shown as not being a real 'bad man' as would be expected of an ex-convict, because he had begged the constable not to shoot.

Task 1

Through Miss Effie and Aunt Sare we learn about two old practices in the community. Try to discover if similar practices existed in your community, and why these practices occurred. Perhaps they still happen? If they no longer happen, why did things change?

'A Story with No Name'

The second chapter speaks of a woman who is in the community, but not really of the community. The 'noname lady', as the narrator calls her, is a member of the wealthy Briscoe family. She is described as having had an upbringing based on ideas of class superiority, which made her see herself as being apart from regular people. Circumstances have changed, but the idea of superiority continues and the villagers themselves accept the separation, careful not to force themselves on the woman. She is apparently ignored by any relatives who still live in Jamaica, including the one who owns the land on which she lives and employs the narrator's father. The woman survives on money sent by those living overseas, and possibly with the interest and help of the narrator's father.

Among the stories about the noname lady is that she used to be an avid and noisy churchgoer in her youth. She had apparently been attracted to and duped by a black man, had become pregnant and aborted the baby, dropped out of church and become silent. She kept to herself, almost a recluse, except for basic human needs that force her to relate to the villagers. Many stories based on superstitions that frightened the child narrator were circulated about the woman and the place where she lived. The 'noname' woman becomes connected to the narrator because the narrator sees her father give the woman the string of cleaned fish he had with him to cook later for his lunch. He said in explanation 'she hungry and I give it to her. I don't want to hear you talking bout this' (page 22). After this, the woman became part of the narrator's nightmare dream experiences in which she felt threatened, and which included a navel string attaching the woman, the narrator and both her parents to each other. The narrator makes further connections between the woman and herself. First, in her curiosity about the woman and her wondering if the woman could speak, she learns from her mother that the woman was 'just strange'. The narrator points out 'I was strange'; 'I understood silence'; 'I did not speak until I was two, they thought I was dumb.'(page

20). This connects to Paul's birth. One story about the woman swelling in the stomach due to supernatural causes eventually resolves itself into her giving birth to a baby boy who becomes the centre of her life. The narrator's mother, waving a weapon, warns a neighbour who suggests a connection between Marlene's father and the 'noname' woman and her child, so silencing a potentially dangerous rumour. The boy did not seem to develop naturally, and when he was eight years he still could not speak, reminding us that the narrator and her brother had been slow to talk in their childhood.

Task 2

The novel hints several times at a social phenomenon in the Caribbean, where many children are born outside of marriage. It also hints at the effects of this feature on the lives of the children. Discuss this with both your Literature teacher and your History teacher. What is the attitude of the villagers to this situation? You will need to look at other stories to answer the question.

'Nathan'

'Nathan' is a character study of the chapter's title character. He is the narrator's brother, the sibling to whom she seems to feel closest. She introduces his character to us by way of little stories which illustrate his deep quietness, his stinginess with words and possessions. The first story is about Nathan, one night finishing his silent preparation for bed, then walking over to his brother and deliberately poking him in the eye. The poke was revenge for some bullying from that brother during the day. Their parents thought the behaviour was justified and even found the incident to be funny. Another later story tells how the adult Nathan, in the quiet and conscientious execution of his duties as a security guard, came to lose a leg and gain financial wealth. He had chosen not to let a politician's demand for special treatment affect his own application of the rules applying to his work. Nathan does not change his lifestyle because he is wealthy – he simply gets a prosthesis, marries, and turns to farming. With a large noisy wife and family, this quiet man is happy.

In this chapter the narrator not only shows why she feels close to Nathan. She helps us to see both his character and her own, so that their differences and similarities are shown. They have always been able to be comfortable together without talking. Among the things she recounts is that they both began to speak relatively late in their childhood, enjoyed each other's company without speech, but also sought quietness apart from each other, and in different ways. Even in the womb they had had similar behaviour, and had affected their mother in similar ways at childbirth. It creates two childhood worlds in the same family, and two adult lives, separate, but supportive.

Task 3

Marlene has several siblings. Why does she choose to focus on Nathan? Discuss your thoughts, and any supporting evidence, with your classmates and teacher.

'The Idiot'

The story starts with a lesson the narrator's mother often tried to teach her children – the need to be respectful in daily dealings with others, and the need to be humble so that life does not find opportunities to embarrass you. The mother uses an example of personal arrogance from her girlhood, and how she had seen herself as being better than a certain man. She had made a point of being haughty with the man, but that man had helped her and saved her life in an act of chivalry. His kind act then and respectful behaviour later had shamed her. The after-effects of that kind act when she considered her own behaviour were difficult for her to bear. She had been conceited enough to see the man previously as trying to 'be fast' with her and she had made it her business never to be pleasant to him. Her memory of the persistent shame whenever she saw that man prompted her to warn her children against such misplaced pride and arrogance.

The narrator's personal challenge – and failure – in being humble comes through a boy called Ezekiel Watkiss and her love for words and success in any activity dealing with the use of words. She was proud of always being at the top of the class. She was just as bright as Wellesley Black, her classmate; but he came to school regularly and was in that class because he was the right age for it, while she had skipped some grades. She did not think that beating him was really remarkable. On the other hand, there was Ezekiel Watkiss, a boy from a large, very poor family. Ezekiel very seldom came to school. In spite of his poor attendance he was not easy to beat. He was unfortunate enough to be seen as ugly, carried the nickname 'hog', and was often jeered at and hit 'accidentally' with stones, by other children. Though he eventually went to the same high school as the narrator, she snubbed him because others did, because he was ugly, and because he was behind her in school. Her high school friends saw him as being less than themselves. She was ashamed to be seen talking to an obvious and unfashionable country boy. In telling of her own lack of humility, Marlene echoes her mother's behaviour of so many years ago:

'I always answered him in carefully chosen monosyllables in my best English, careful as my mother
in her best courthouse voice, my head flung up like
queen and my mouth pursed up like suck orange and
I giving out largesse.' (page 52)

She was shocked one day to find herself unable to find a response
to his crisp standard English challenge, when she acted snootily
to him: 'I am not less than you, you know, Marlene' (page 53).
In adulthood, while the narrator is still trying to find her place,
Ezekiel Watkiss, who had known real poverty, had moved on to
become a successful and wealthy contractor, and a recurring
memory to cause Marlene some discomfort about the way she
had treated him. The story ends with a feeling that the narrator
regrets not having dealt better with Ezekiel Watkiss.

It is in this chapter that we hear the narrator's name for
the first time, and it is called by Ezekiel, someone who perhaps
challenges her to be her true self, since she is by now, in the
collection of stories, old enough and experienced enough to have
a mind of her own. By the end of the story, the narrator is looking
back from adulthood on the way we fail to see real people behind
the social stereotype. Her conclusion suggests that we often deny
ourselves the opportunity to be part of something good.

Task 4

This story starts with three Caribbean proverbs. Try to find
explanations for these by discussing them with older people.
Trace how they apply in the story.

'Miss Minnie'

Miss Minnie is a story about family and family relationships, about difficult relationships and the role of silence in shaping perceptions, reactions and such relationships. The story is primarily about the kind of parental relationship which develops between a child, whose biological mother abandons him in babyhood, and the woman who raises him. A major focus in the story is the value of communication. The relationships are complicated by the father's uncommunicative attitude to Minnie, a replacement wife for the woman who had left him, and the way Minnie and the child need to depend on each other, though their own verbal communication is little. It is actually a story in which silence (lack of communication) can create a variety of potentially destructive problems: jealousy, resentment, fear, distrust. Silence also hides deep love which the characters are unable to express. It seems that when the two major characters, Miss Minnie and Raymond, move away from the practical country environment where the emphasis is on struggle and survival, that they are better able to let their feelings show, particularly when each feels threatened by the re-entry of Raymond's natural mother into his life. Raymond learns how to accept both women into his life and still make Miss Minnie know that she is not replaceable. Raymond's efforts to make Miss Minnie comfortable in the village illustrate how the move of the younger generation into the city affects development and change in the village.

'Morris Hole'

The story 'Morris Hole' is not one story, but a collection of separate recollections which speak directly about the narrator's life. Morris Hole refers to the place on the river which the villagers made their own for washing, and for fun. The narrator tries to show how the river awakens memories of innocent childhood fun like skating down the gully, or walking in puddles to hear the squishing noises, waiting for the mist to lift so she could enjoy the first feel of cold river water, or playing free and naked in the river. This spot allowed her to look to the horizon where the small river joined the large sea, and to spark visions of the future for her. Ironically, the river is larger at Morris Hole than what she can see of the ocean in the distance, but this does not reduce her determination to go towards that horizon. She also tries to share the most terrible moment of her life when, because of a neighbour's careless words, her growing femininity is held against her and her mother stops her free behaviour and enjoyment of the river.

The story also looks at the family genealogy: Marlene's mother remembers with disgust how her grandmother named the wrong father for her son, and the narrator remembers the unpleasant but unavoidable experience of going to speak to a paternal grandfather who never acknowledged her and her siblings. The narrator's adult voice has a moment of self-examination as she puts these bits and pieces of her life together. Marlene muses that 'a shrink' would say she had put what, to her, were distasteful stories of her genealogy alongside the story of herself entering puberty, because both experiences were uncomfortable and embarrassing. They would say she had used the river symbolically, since the river represents life, connects her with her ancestor as they both lived there within its influence, because of the symbolic value of the river as being female, and because of the folklore of the of the rivermumma and sexuality. Her response is to deny any of that educated approach; she was simply telling a story the way that was natural. In her own words: "that is how we tell a story where I come from, it don't haffi come

211

straight for else it not sweet, and is just so it go' (page 102). She is determined not to change anything, however, confessing that her story is told the way it is because mixing it up adds interest: 'it don't haffi come straight for else it not sweet ... '(page 102).

Task 5

Make a list of significant experiences or observations the narrator makes in connection with the river, and at what stages in her life she makes these observations.

'Travellers, or Fathers, or Little Fool-Fool'

This story introduces the concept of the migrant itinerant labourer – the people who, alone or with family, took all their portable possessions and walked to new areas in search of work. Some settled and grew into the village, others moved on. For some of these travellers it was common practice to establish some family connection in the area. The narrator lets the voices of the villagers tell the story of such introductions and settlements. However, not all travellers had, or created, the roots that made them real. Cudjoe Man and Long Man each represented one of these types.

At the end of the story it is clear that Marlene has thought about the events and has compared Long Man with Cudjoe Man. Her imaginative mind has created ideas to fuel fear. The source of Marlene's fear is summed up after she tells these men's stories when she reminds us of

> 'old wives' tales and black people gossip and old naygar goat mouth that said travellers sometimes never came back'. (pages 137–8)

She first describes an image from her very young imagination and memory, a travelling worker called Long Man. The narrator admits to not really remembering Long Man as a person, but she creates through him one extreme of the travellers, a man who

> 'lived not in places but in the spaces in between … in the indeterminate space between the highroads and unexpecting shelters'. (pages 106–7)

He lived without responsibility for others and his departure left no sorrow. He is the opposite of the next character, Cudjoe Man, who also came through as an itinerant, but one with responsibilities.

Cudjoe Man decided to stay for the sake of his retarded child. Villagers called her 'Little Fool-Fool' but accepted her in the community. The resemblance between Cudjoe Man and his daughter, as well as his attachment to her, evokes the telling of some folk wisdom about children's resemblance to their parents. Cudjoe Man puts his loved and pampered daughter, who is always smiling, into school, dressing her well and insisting that she be treated with respect. Cudjoe man dealt firmly with the school and the children, and violently stopped interference from others who spread malicious insinuations or tried to molest his girl. Though he looked for female companionship, and women admired him for himself and the way he looked after his daughter, Cudjoe Man did not take a woman into his home because of a possible threat to the girl. The village knew him to have an established relationship with a pleasant but plain girl called Dottie, but secret teasing and sexual byplay between him and Minna had also been observed.

There is a confrontation between these two women who vie for Cudjoe Man's attention. Unfortunately for Minna, the more popular and saucier of the two women, Samson, the man with whom she lives, regards her as being his property. The murderously jealous Samson brutally beats and disfigures Minna after he learns about the women's confrontation. Though the neighbours try to keep the cutlass-carrying Cudjoe Man away from Samson, his pain at seeing what has been done to Minna is such that he attacks Samson. There is no stated conclusion on what Cudjoe Man does or of Samson's fate. There is not even a judgement from the villagers, but Cudjoe Man went to jail and his relatives came and took the girl away. Noticeably, as she looked back from the car, she was not smiling.

The narrator attempts to explain why the stories of these two men surface in her mind. Long Man had last come to visit after Cudjoe Man was taken away, but it was Cudjoe Man's memory that was stronger because he left behind people to whom he had been real, who cared about the real man he was to his daughter and others, and the experiences he had had were real. Unlike her description of Long Man, the narrator does not need to resort to fantasy. It seems that the contemplation is spurred by, or itself spurred thoughts on, the close relationship she had with her father (pages 137–8), a real man 'who made dents on anything he sat on'. He too sometimes travelled for work as the other two men had done, and could be gone for weeks. During this time she looked for him every evening. Her worry was so strong that she had nightmares, culminating in one where her father was believed lost at sea, and her mother had gone to his memorial service, while she, Marlene, refused to accept that he was not returning.

Task 6

(a) Marlene's experiences with her father may not be very different from Little Fool-Fool's experiences. Think about it and note the similarities and differences.

(b) As with the story 'The Idiot' Marlene may have made a connection between the title and herself in 'Travellers, or Fathers, or Little Fool-Fool'. Write down your thoughts on this for later discussion.

(c) In telling about Long Man, Marlene mentions her mother's name for the first time (page 106). What other observations does she make about Long Man and her parents that suggest she thought a lot about his visits?

'So Few and Such Morning Songs'

Mr Papacita is the village singer, a sort of Pied Piper able to draw all the children in with his vibrant singing. The narrator equates his songs with bright colours and the rainbow. He is a happy, hardworking man who seizes every opportunity to sing, usually ribald songs, on a daily basis, but he has an excellent voice and considerable versatility. Singing is very much a part of his personality, and at weddings it seems to affect him in the same way Miss Effie's announcing affects her – he is taken over by the music. On all occasions his singing brings happiness to everyone around. His story introduces all sorts of occasions for music, and all sorts of instruments. His wife, who is an avid Church of God member, decides not to nag him into joining the church. The people find it interesting that, despite their many years of marriage, Papacita and his wife remain very good friends and playmates. Several other church women and the pastor try to seduce him into church, but he makes jokes about all of them.

When his wife and best friend dies suddenly, the funeral service ironically becomes another occasion for lusty singing and instrumental sounds, but Mr Papacita leaves the service. Mr Papacita's life changes: He is angry with his wife for dying; he still sings, but his main song is now 'One a dese fine fine time …Ah go bruk down de house … an g'way!' He now often wakes the village with this hangover-inspired song, or stumbles drunkenly home to its refrain. He no longer plays any of the instruments, saying: 'right now the instrument want tune'. He deteriorates badly, drinking all day and sometimes doing a kind of preaching on the street corner. He collapses one day and is hospitalized. When Papacita recovers, he no longer drinks or sings, and rejects the attempts of the people from his wife's former church to pray for him. He goes into a sort of silence which is very different from the angry noisiness that followed immediately on his wife's death. One day he inexplicably walks into the Wesleyan church and is later baptized. He remains a staunch member thereafter, breaking the silence and singing with the same passion as before.

216

However, according to the narrator, he sings songs in the lower tones of the colour spectrum: blues, black and white and purple, not the bright oranges and reds as previously. The narrator finds the change confusing, and the story ends with a silence as she has decided to 'wait and see'.

Task 7

What contribution did Mr Papacita make to the village? Using his story:
  (a) list the different attitudes to church and religion held in the community.
  (b) What community events/activities provided recreation and entertainment for the community?

Task 8

  1. Consider, for instance, Marlene's narration about the family friend, Long Man (see pages 106–11). Make a list of any particular features she describes. Make notes which will help you in a discussion on the value of this character in the novel. This can be done to help yourself to develop a bank of details to strengthen your discussions.

Task 9

  2. Marlene gives no details about her parents' appearance, nor does she make any judgements of them. However, we do get a picture of how very important they are in her life, and to the family. After you have read the novel carefully on your own, work in groups to complete the following extended lists. Note things done and said, as well as those not done/said:

- The relationship between the parents
- The mother:
  - her role/activities in the family
  - her behaviour as a villager
  - things she taught the children
- The father: as above for the mother.

Consider why, in 'A Story with No Name' the narrator's mother silences the villager who makes insinuations about her husband.

GUIDELINES FOR EXAM PREPARATION

Penetrating the novel

Most times when you study literature you do it because you are expected to, and then you remember the contents of a book only as a story, or you have difficulty remembering. You can help yourself to enjoy the activity, and to be able to understand and remember the contents if you try to relate what you read to your life. Ask yourself questions like this:

- Does this remind me of anything I have heard in a History or Social Studies class?
- What in this work makes me remember the movie I saw … ?
- Did I hear something on the news which sounds like an event in the work?
- What are the things here that make me think they sound like part of my life (or my parents' life)?

After you have read and understood the contents of the novel, you might ask other questions, such as: what is the writer's intention/purpose?; Should I take all of this literally?; Does a particular thing mean more than it seems on the surface? You can think of similar questions which will help you to focus and penetrate the novel or play.

Answering CSEC-style questions

It seems that questions are never 'only questions'. Questions also give us information. For instance, if you were asked to comment on the relationship between Marlene and her siblings before she went to secondary school, using *Songs of Silence*, you would need to read the question thoughtfully. You would recognize the use of the plural noun 'siblings', and so (i) realize that you would have been given information directly – Marlene had siblings; (ii) because of the shape of the question you would recognize the suggestion that you had to find out how many siblings there were, what gender, whether they were older or younger. You would, in short, have to analyse the question to find out what it gave, what it suggested, what it wanted and even how much it wanted.

Sometimes the instructions could indicate: *write an essay* … . In such a case, you would remember to (i) create an introduction which gives the background for your answer, and suggests what points (information) you will examine; (ii) follow this with a number of paragraphs, each of which develops one of the points you indicated in your introduction, being careful to connect ideas, and to put them in a sensible order; (iii) conclude the essay by perhaps evaluating the situation, connecting the relevant aspects of the novel with reality, or some suitable ending.

Other questions break up what is needed into sections. Generally this is still like the essay, in that each section takes you further in your treatment of the content. Still others ask you to relate to the writer's craft, to say how and why a thing is done, and with what effects. There are also those questions which invite you to compare and contrast two works from different places and cultures, to discuss how they respond to the same things. Following are two different kinds of questions and possible outlines.

Short questions

In the 1960s world of *Songs of Silence* it is recognized that education is necessary, but different for girls and boys.

(a) What details about the system of education in rural Jamaica do we learn through Marlene? (9 marks)

(b) By what strategies does the author help us to understand the kind of education she received and her learning environment? (8 marks)

(c) How does the story 'The Idiot' illustrate the social value of education? (8 marks)

Possible notes for your answer

(a) Aspects of the education system to discuss include the following:
- Primary schools were located in each district
- Children walked to school
- Girls were sent to school more than boys
- Children could be sent to any school which satisfied the parents
- Flogging (the strap) was utilized in some schools
- The content was often foreign to the students' lived experiences
- Boys were often at a disadvantage in the classroom
- The pupil-teacher system was used
- Children could spend several years in the same class
- Agriculture was part of the primary school curriculum
- Some children did not go beyond primary school.

(b) The author reveals information about the type of education and the school environment with the following 'clues':
- The author has Marlene quote from the books used:

  'Othere the old sea captain who dwelt in Heligo land ... '; ' ... dry clashed his harness in the icy caves and barren chasms' and songs ' ... half a poun fipenny rice half a poun a weevil' (page 43).

- The audience is able to recognize other features, such as that the extra-curricular activities (Girl Guides, Brownies) were British, and the songs the children sang were from other parts of the British Empire ('Waltzing Matilda'). (See page 92.)
- She has people make comments. Marlene asked about boys' school attendance and her mother commented:

  'I use to wonder why boys like Bas just didn't stay

221

away on Thursdays rather than going through all the shame ... But my mother said ... (page 45).

Miss Minnie did not let Raymond stop going to school because ' ... go to school, finish you education and get a good job so you can hol up your head ... ' (page 60).

(c) 'The Idiot' helps us to experience several details that showed the value of education:
   - Students were not taught about themselves.
   - Agriculture or 'farm projects' as the narrator called it, helped to maintain a regard for farming in the rural district.
   - Failure to excel at book-based activities was not seen as a problem or weakness. (See the earlier explanation given by Marlene's mother.)
   - Book knowledge was more important than understanding – in primary school the narrator was given the facts about bauxite but did not know what it was (page 46). In secondary school she read and enjoyed *Lorna Doon* (page 49) and did not know why she saw a similarity between that character and Ezekiel Watkiss's tall, beautiful sister.

Extended question

Choose a character from *Songs of Silence* whose story illustrates the need to deal with struggle against some difficulty. Consider the extent to which the character succeeds or fails. Show how and why the character succeeds or fails in the response to the challenge. Compare this character's experiences with those of another character facing challenges in another text from a different cultural background.

Possible notes for your answer

In order to respond successfully to this question, you should do the following:
- Introduce the works by name, and the characters you will use in the discussion.
- For each character, summarize the peculiar situation on which you will focus, being careful to show why it is a challenge.
- Give a description of any significant actions.
- Consider the outcome and assess whether all or part was successful.
- Compare the strengths and/or weaknesses of the characters (those strengths or weaknesses which relate to the particular challenge) and the decisions taken in each case.
- What reasons would you offer as causing the success or failure in the case of each character?

NB: Some students are more comfortable if they write all they need to on one text and its character, then the other. Other students are comfortable handling characters simultaneously. Choose the strategy with which you feel comfortable. Make a simple outline, and be sure to check it frequently to ensure that you are answering all aspects of the question for each character. Make sure you think about the characters you want to pair, to be sure they are suitable together.

For this question Cudjoe Man and Ezekiel Watkiss are suitable choices. Other possibilities include Raymond's father, Lester; Raymond; Mr Papacita.

Cudjoe Man needed to look after the welfare of his mentally retarded daughter. His intention was to make her feel secure and loved, and to protect her from callous or careless people. His challenges included finding a pleasant social environment, a suitable school, and paid employment. He found these in Baltree District. Consider the following:

- How do we feel about Cudjoe Man and why?
- What steps does Cudjoe Man take for his daughter's welfare and why?
- What of his own needs?
- Are there any elements that complicate or otherwise affect his actions?
- Why does he react as he does to Minna's injuries?
- When he reacts to Minna's situation, does the writer influence us in how we feel about him? If so, how?
- What effect, if any, does Cudjoe Man's daughter's departure with relatives have on our reaction to Cudjoe Man?
- Has he succeeded in meeting the challenge?

Support your answer

Ezekiel Watkiss had to struggle against his poverty and people's perception of and reaction to him. He had to make up for inadequate schooling. His lack of good looks made him more of a target, when one considers that his sister who was also poor, but was beautiful, was not made to suffer. His challenge was a perception that origin or class limited development. Ezekiel had more strengths than weaknesses – he was bright at school though he did not attend often; he was patient; he was determined. His challenge was to get Marlene to talk with him and to respect him. Marlene resisted or insulted him (she behaved like a snob, felt superior to him, was embarrassed by his quality of dress, and most of all, wanted to be accepted by the 'in-crowd' at school).

Consider Ezekiel's reactions to those who tormented him.
- Did he show cowardice or strength?
- What circumstances worked for or against him?
- What about Ezekiel made Marlene regret her treatment of him?
- What quality (qualities) could have brought him the success Marlene identified him as having gained?

Remember that this kind of question is complete only after you have applied similar treatment to the other literary work.